NEWCOMER'S HANDBOOK™

FOR
Minneapolis SaintPaul

NEWCOMER'S HANDBOOK™

FOR
Minneapolis SaintPaul

Minnesota
WELCOME
10,000 Lakes

FIRST BOOKS

P.O. Box 578147
Chicago, IL 60657
773-276-5911
http://www.firstbooks.com

Author: Maris Strautmanis
Publisher and Editor: Jeremy Solomon
Associate Editor: Bernadette Duperron
Cover Design: Miles DeCoster, Art Machine, Inc.
Production: Gale DeCoster, Amber Mintz, Art Machine, Inc.
Map: Gale DeCoster, Art Machine, Inc.

ISBN 0-912301-33-3

ISSN 1087-8467

Manufactured in the United States of America.

Published by First Books, Inc., P.O. Box 578147, Chicago, IL 60657, 773-276-5911.

Welcome to Minneapolis and St. Paul, the Twin Cities, one of the most livable urban areas in the United States. Now put on some warmer clothes! Living in Minneapolis or St. Paul does mean enduring long, harsh winters. But if it's your first venture north, don't despair. There's much more to the Twin Cities than the season of ice. In fact, the summers here are warm and lush. And since it's the contrasts that often bring beauty to light, you are likely to find beauty in the dramatic change in seasons. There's more: the people are genuinely friendly, Twin Cities streets are actually clean (littering is, delightfully, still frowned upon here), lakes and woods dot the metro area, and many of these natural oases are connected by parkways. There are world-famous art museums, music ensembles, and theater companies. In fact, there's so much to enjoy here, you may soon be tempted to throw up your hat on the street, like TV's Mary Tyler Moore. She was onto something, you know.

Wherever you decide to live, you won't be far from a lake, river or park (there are 6,400 acres of parks and lakes in the metro area). Early on, city leaders wisely set aside virtually all shoreline land in the Twin Cities as public property. The park lands along lakes and rivers are connected by parkways—one-way streets following the shoreline, often including bicycle and walking paths. People use the parks all year, and winter actually adds to their quality and beauty. There's nothing quite like cross country skiing by moonlight over a frozen lake, and a hot bowl of soup afterwards. Then in the summer, you can canoe on the same lake. Those contrasts!

A perennially popular topic of conversation among Twin Cities boosters is the strong economy here. In the 1850s, the area became a boomtown in the true sense of the word, when Minneapolis entrepreneurs built huge wooden booms across the Mississippi River to haul in logs being sent downstream by logging companies. That kind of enterprising vigor still exists today. Successful corporations of all sizes in virtually all industries have sprung up or settled here and made the metro area, next to Chicago, the second economic center of the upper Midwest. Other factors add to the availability and stability of jobs: the Minnesota state capitol and state offices are in St. Paul, and the massive University of Minnesota's main campus is in Minneapolis. Unemployment in the Twin Cities has happily remained a few points below the national average for over a decade. Recently, a ReliaStar Financial study of the 100 largest metropolitan areas in the U.S. ranked Minneapolis/St. Paul second best in the nation in terms of "financial security" as determined by such factors as unemployment, housing costs, household income, education, and participation in retirement savings plans.

Chances are you'll find rents, house prices, and the general cost of living low, especially if you're coming from another major city. The flipside of this, however, is that incomes here lag slightly behind those in other metropolitan areas. But, as Twin Cities chauvinists like to point out, the low cost of living means that real household income—the amount you get to spend on Rollerblades®, Guthrie tickets, or crocus bulbs—is among the highest of any city in the nation.

Although the two Twin Cities comprise one metropolitan area, and lines between them are in many ways blurred, residents like to think of their identities as distinct. Downtown Minneapolis is ten miles west of downtown St. Paul, but more than distance separates them. St. Paul (1994 population: 271,660) is viewed as the quieter city; Minneapolis (366,480) is thought to be more urban, with more typically urban problems as well. Residents argue over which city has more culture and quality of life. Once you move here, you can make your own judgment about these reputations.

It is true that there are many flaxen-haired and fair skinned people here, yet the Twin Cities are a center for ethnic groups besides the well-known Scandinavians and Germans. African-Americans make up about 13 percent of Minneapolis and eight percent of St. Paul. Also, St. Paul has a sizeable Hispanic neighborhood. The largest urban Native American population in the U.S. is centered in Minneapolis. The country's largest population of Hmong Americans, an ethnic subgroup from Southeast Asia, numbers some 20,000 in St. Paul and 10,000 in Minneapolis. Also, the Twin Cities are a major center for Tibetan refugees.

The people are what many give as the real reason for the high quality of life here. Folks tend to say 'hello' to strangers and do what they can to make a newcomer comfortable. Make no mistake, there are all kinds of people here just as everywhere, and "Minnesota Nice" doesn't appear to extend onto the freeways. Lake Wobegon, the fictitious world of St. Paul writer Garrison Keillor, is a little outdated, and the frightening world of the film *Fargo* is nothing more than the over stimulation of the filmmaker's imagination. But you probably will notice a sturdy determination by Minnesotans to make life tolerable, even pleasant, for each other. You might be confused at first and not believe it, but don't take it personally. People here do mean it; they want to be nice.

History

If you drive around Minnesota, you'll notice the rolling, sloping terrain, completely flattened in some places. The gentle grade of the land is the result of a series of natural events that have taken place over the eons. Hundreds of millions of years ago, a sea covered large regions of the state, including everything south of the Twin Cities and Minnesota's northwestern corner. This ancient sea left deep deposits of sandstone, limestone and shale (today, an abundant source of ground water). Much more recently, geologically speaking, a series of ice ages swept up and down Minnesota, scraping and rearranging the face of the land. The last glaciers receded approximately ten thousand years ago, leaving gentling undulating ridges and valleys as well as the thousands of lakes Minnesota is famous for.

Native American tribes hunted and migrated over the rolling hills of Minnesota for centuries before the Europeans arrived. One of the area's earliest known place names was Im-in-i-ja Ska, given to the tall white sandstone bluff that creates a sharp curve in the Mississippi at the center of St. Paul. The first extensive description of the region by a European was written in 1683 by Father Louis Hennepin, a Franciscan adventurer who traveled with a party of Dakota guides up the river to a wide falls, which he named St. Anthony Falls. Hennepin was standing smack in the center of what is now downtown Minneapolis.

The U.S. Cavalry made expeditions to the Upper Midwest at the turn of the nineteenth century to see what they had gained in the Louisiana Purchase. Lieutenant Zebulon Pike found two different groups of Native American tribes living here, the Ojibwe and the Dakota. Pike signed an agreement with Little Crow, a Dakota, in 1803 that ceded to the U.S. nine square miles of land at the confluence of the Mississippi and Minnesota Rivers, where he built Fort Snelling.

Fur traders, farmers and others settled down river from the fort. An earnest missionary named Lucien Galtier built a log church in 1841, and named it after St. Paul, the Apostle of Nations. The name stuck for the settlement.

Entrepreneurs also moved up river to St. Anthony Falls. They used the hydraulic power of the Mississippi to mill flour and saw lumber. The nickname "Mill City" for Minneapolis comes from Minneapolis' milling days. This settlement, on the east bank of the river, was known as St. Anthony, but Charles Hoag, a teacher, proposed a different name for it, combining Minne, the Dakota word for "water," and polis, the Greek word for "city." That name—Minneapolis—came into use as the city grew. The Main Street of old St. Anthony has been preserved as Saint Anthony Main, a shopping and entertainment district downtown on the east bank of the river.

Relations between the thriving white settlements and Native Americans in the area were not always harmonious. There was an agreement by the U.S. to send food and supplies to displaced Indians, but during a recession in 1862, federal food rations were not sent. A group of hungry and desperate Indians raided a homestead and killed the people living there. More violence followed, leading to the Dakota War of 1862. When the fighting ended, thirty-eight Dakotas were selected at random and executed by hanging.

Both cities went through booms in the late 19th century as waves of immigrants moved to the New World. In 1867 Minneapolis was incorporated as a city, though, at first St. Paul was the larger of the two competing hamlets. During the 1880s, however, Minneapolis began to overtake its neighbor both in population and commerce. Rivalry between the cities was fierce, and led to the Great Census War of 1890. The first census results showed that Minneapolis was population champ, but St. Paul officials charged fraud, and a scandal ensued. A deputy U.S. marshal arrested census workers in downtown Minneapolis and results were recounted. Investigators found that counters in both cities had inflated numbers with "residents" living in cemeteries and office buildings. The recount confirmed that Minneapolis had more residents, and it has remained the larger city ever since.

Although St. Paul has gradually garnered the reputation as the sleepier town, it hasn't always been that way. During Prohibition from 1920–1933, mobsters running liquor from Canada brought their ill-gotten gains and their wild ways to the city of St. Paul. Arrests and indictments in the late 1930s led to the end of St. Paul's "gangster city" era.

Both cities continued to grow, particularly after World War II. As the suburbs and the interstate system took shape in the 1950s, a regional governing body, now known as the Metropolitan Council, was formed in 1957 to manage development problems such as sewer and water service. In the 1970s, there was new growth in both cities. The construction of the Investors Diversified Services (IDS) building in Minneapolis signaled the emergence of Minneapolis as a financial center for the upper Midwest. Many downtown buildings both in Minneapolis and St. Paul were connected with indoor above-ground skyways to make living and working easier during the long, often bitter months of winter.

It was at this time that many investors and government officials also became concerned with preserving more of the original buildings that still remained in the cities. Numerous restoration projects came about including the Landmark Center in St. Paul and the Warehouse District in Minneapolis. Fortunately, these initiatives have kept alive some of the early history of the two boomtowns on the upper Mississippi River as they continue to expand ever outward.

In the 1990s, neighborhood revitalization is a driving force in the core Twin Cities. Every neighborhood organization in Minneapolis now receives city funding to develop long-range priorities for improvements, and both cities have aggressive initiatives to raze or rehabilitate boarded-up property. In 1994, several government agencies signed an agreement designed to protect the water quality of the lakes in Minneapolis. City leaders hope strategies such as these will allow the Twin Cities to remain vital and pleasant places in which to live.

What to bring

- A car, probably, and one that's in shape to take on winter. The Twin Cities' bus system, which goes by the clunky title of Metropolitan Council Transit Operations (MCTO), has been struggling to keep up with the fast growth of outer-ring suburbs (it now offers express connections to several suburbs). Plans for a light rail commuter system have been discussed for years but, unfortunately, never followed through on. If you don't drive a car, though, you certainly won't be alone; about one-third of all Twin Cities residents get to work either by bus, bike, carpool, foot or cross-country skis. If you do bring a car, make sure you get it "winterized" and ready for extended periods of sub-zero weather. For more information, see the chapter, **Surviving Winter.**

- A map. There are places where Twin Cities streets and highways follow a perfect grid, and places where streets are laid out at crazy angles to the grid. This guide will help you to get to know the neighborhoods, but for the full picture, you'll need to accompany it with a map.

- Warm clothes. No kidding, you'll need them. Get a serious winter coat (preferably down-lined), substantial sweaters, and boots, and also, consider buying a down-filled quilt to use on your bed. It will make a world of difference in terms of how enjoyable (or painful) your winter will be. Stocking up on rugged winterwear is made easier by the fact that Minnesota does not charge sales tax on apparel.

Most importantly, bring an open mind and positive attitude. If this is your first experience in the upper Midwest, prepare for peculiarities such as lutefisk and the all-purpose, one-word answer, "yah." And while people here are often friendlier than in most urban areas they can at the same time be more reserved in demeanor than in other parts of the country. Attempts are made throughout this guide to describe the fine qualities to be found here, but you will do the best discovering yourself.
    Welcome!

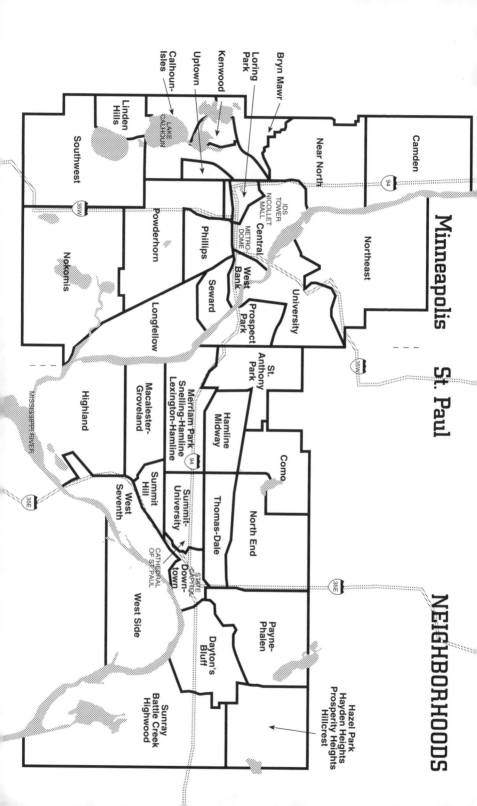

Minneapolis   St. Paul   NEIGHBORHOODS

Perhaps the most important information a newcomer to the Twin Cities needs is a knowledge of the neighborhoods. Moving companies you can find in the Yellow Pages, but where can you learn about the many possible areas in which you could live? Read on! There are twenty-eight distinct neighborhoods in the Twin Cities, including a number of smaller historic or otherwise unique districts. Summit Hill in St. Paul is a row of 19th-century mansions with historic character; downtown Minneapolis has shiny new townhouses and renovated warehouse lofts; Linden Hills in South Minneapolis offers single-family bungalows with tree-shaded yards. No "Most Recommended" list is given here; most neighborhoods in Minneapolis or St. Paul are fine places for a newcomer to move. Everybody has different needs, though, and the following neighborhood descriptions should help direct you to places that match yours.

As you explore the Twin Cities, you may notice certain types of housing cropping up again and again. The Midwestern square is a style you will see throughout Minneapolis-St. Paul. These simple houses, consisting of a two-story wood structure with a front porch, dormer windows, and high ceilings, date to the turn of the century, and many have been split into duplexes. Arts-and-Crafts style bungalows, often with stucco siding, were mostly built in the 1910s to 1930s and are common on the quieter streets close to the edges of both cities. Typically, the bungalows have handsome hardwood built-in buffets and window seats. Near Lake Harriet and Lake of the Isles, you will find Prairie-style houses. These low-lying, natural wood and stone houses with narrow windows, pioneered by Frank Lloyd Wright early in this century, are distinctly Midwestern. Colonials, two-story box-like houses with symmetrically arranged windows and a central door, line many older streets of the inner city such as Pillsbury Avenue in Minneapolis. You will also see many Tudors in older neighborhoods. They are the houses with steep roofs and sides decorated with dark wood timbers and stone arches. Some Tudor-style houses were built as recently as the 1940s. Finally, grandiose Victorian wood-frame houses, dating to the late 19th century and adorned with gables, towers and outside woodwork, stand out in older neighborhoods.

Victorian-era houses can also look quite plain, with only a small wooden decoration under the eaves and a tall front porch.

People here identify strongly with their neighborhoods. When asked where they live, residents in Minneapolis and St. Paul are more likely to give the name of their neighborhood than a street address. Neighborhood newspapers are published in many areas, and are often available free of charge at newsstands, cafes, and convenience stores. Pick up a neighborhood paper to get a sense of current issues in the area, and you may also find helpful apartment listings. Virtually every neighborhood is represented by a neighborhood organization. These organizations are an important source of information and advice when hunting for an apartment, and they can also help you become familiar with your new community once you've moved in. The telephone numbers of neighborhood organizations are listed after the description of each community.

The number of the police precinct serving the area is also listed; however, if you are in any emergency situation, call 911. The precinct stations don't dispatch officers, and you'll save a step by calling 911 yourself. For general questions about safety, a good place to check is the neighborhood organization. The folks at these organizations are in tune with what's going on in their neighborhood because they live there.

Crime rates in the Twin Cities have remained level in recent years, particularly for "stranger-on-stranger" crimes. Even so, Minneapolis and St. Paul do have their share of crime. Suburbs are also not immune, particularly to property crimes. Just as in any other metropolitan area, pay attention to your "spider sense," and do your best to avoid any situation that makes you uncomfortable. Pay attention to activity at least a block away in both directions, put money, credit cards and keys in a clothing pocket, and, above all, keep your eyes and ears open.

Boundaries shown for neighborhoods are the same ones used by city planners and the newspapers' classified ads, which should make this book easy to use when house hunting. A note: you can reach the U.S. Postal Service through one central metro area number, the Customer Information Service, at 349-4711. People at this office can answer your questions, or connect you to a branch location. This number is listed again at the end of each neighborhood profile, along with branch office locations, zip codes, area code, bus lines, nearby library branches, hospitals and everything else you need to know to get settled in your new neighborhood.

MINNEAPOLIS

A city promotional brochure describes the larger of the Twin Cities as "cozy neighborhoods, big city energy." Minneapolis (1994 population: 366,480) has shrunk a bit from its peak population of 550,000 residents in the 1950s, mostly because of suburban flight. But don't take this as a sign of urban decay. Minneapolis has a pleasing combination of urban energy and down home tranquillity that will always attract people. The skyline is graceful, the streets hum with energy, the economy and culture are international. But at the same time, the places where people live in Minneapolis are down-to-earth and well-tended. Many neighborhoods have city-commissioned gateways, sculptures that welcome visitors and symbolize neighborhood pride.

Local government has taken an active role in keeping up the quality of Minneapolis' neighborhoods. Since 1990, the Neighborhood Revitalization Program, or NRP has funded neighborhood groups and helped them put together long-range plans for the communities in which they live, giving the neighborhoods a direct voice in city planning. Another city initiative, the Minneapolis Community Development Agency (MCDA), funds large-scale commercial projects and also offers low-rate loans for home overhauls.

There are eleven communities in Minneapolis, each of which is described in the following section. Within these eleven communities are eighty-one separate neighborhoods, which are listed with each community (some well-known ones are described further).

Central

Downtown East
Downtown West
Elliot Park

Loring Park
North Loop
Stevens Square/Loring Heights

Boundaries: North: Plymouth Ave., Mississippi River. **West:** I-94. **South:** Franklin Ave., Highway 12. **East:** I-35W.

The Central community consists of downtown Minneapolis plus four surrounding neighborhoods, including Loring Park. A key feature of downtown living is easy access—to a job, city offices, the Central Library, shopping and entertainment. You're also not far from a relaxing walk along the river or through Loring Park.

Downtown West centers around Nicollet Mall, an eight-block commercial strip closed off to cars, and the restored Warehouse District, an area of nightclubs that follows First Avenue north of the Target Center. Watch for artist-designed bus shelters and benches in these areas. Downtown West is lined with plenty of hi-rise apartment buildings, as well as luxury suites and condominiums. Overbuilding here forced developers in the 1980s to convert condominiums into more affordable rental apartments. Also, loft apartments have been created out of 19th century industrial buildings in the Warehouse District. Four-story brick apartments in the Stevens Square and Elliot Park neighborhoods are more affordable, but adjacent to Interstate 94.

Loring Park

Lovely turn-of-the-century brick walk-up apartments and large stone houses surround Loring Park, with its pond, shuffleboard courts and summer movies sponsored by the Walker Art Center. An air of grandeur in Loring Park is enhanced by the Basilica of St. Mary and Hennepin Avenue United Methodist Church.

Loring Park residents are an eclectic mix of professionals, artists, and students. Also, this area has been a popular residential choice among the gay community. Minneapolis Community College borders the East side of the park. The staff of the *Utne Reader,* an alternative news digest, regularly get together in the Loring Cafe. The Red Eye Collaboration, Loring Playhouse, Walker Art Center and Guthrie Theater are all nearby. If you live in Loring Park, you'll never wonder where to go for food, entertainment or just meeting people.

Area Code: 612

Zip Codes: 55402, 55403, 55404, 55405, 55411, 55415

Post Offices: Main Office, 110 South 1st St. Loop Station, 110 South 8th St. Loring Station, 18 North 12th St. Butler Quarter Station, 100 North 6th St. Commerce Station, 307 4th Ave. South. (All post office branches can be reached at 349-4711.)

Police Precinct: 4th, 1925 Plymouth Ave. North, 673-5704.

Emergency Hospital: Hennepin County Medical Center, 701 Park Ave. South, 347-2121.

Library: Central Library, 300 Nicollet Mall, 372-6500.

Bus Lines: Most city bus routes pass through downtown Minneapolis. You can get around Downtown by bus on any major street, and Downtown fares are reduced. Check a transit map (a transit store at 719 Marquette Ave. gives them out) or call 373-3333. **94B, C, D Express**: 6th St./I-94 to downtown St. Paul.

Neighborhood Organizations:
Downtown Minneapolis Residents Association (Downtown East/West, North Loop), 220-3836.
Elliot Park Neighborhood, Inc., 335-5846.
Citizens for Loring Park Community, 673-9518.
Stevens Square Community Organization, 871-7307.

Calhoun/Isles

Bryn Mawr
Calhoun
Cedar-Isles-Dean
East Calhoun
East Isles

Kenwood
Lowry Hill
Lowry Hill East
West Calhoun
Uptown

Boundaries: North: Bassett Creek. **West:** France Ave. **South:** 38th St. **East:** Lyndale Ave.

The neighborhoods around Lake Calhoun, Lake of the Isles and Cedar Lake were the first to be settled after Downtown, and the city's first trolleys ran from Downtown to these neighborhoods. It's easy to see why—living near the lakes brings a certain measure of peace to your daily grind. The Calhoun-Isles community is still one of the most popular places for newcomers to settle.

The area can be divided into three distinct communities. To the east: the trendy, populous neighborhoods commonly known as Uptown include Lowry Hill, Lowry Hill East (also known as the Wedge), Calhoun, and East Calhoun. To the west: the meandering streets of Bryn Mawr, Cedar-Isles-Dean and West Calhoun offer affordable housing near the lakes. Bordering the north shore of Lake of the Isles, Kenwood is one of the most expensive neighborhoods in the Twin Cities.

Uptown spreads outward from Calhoun Square, with a mall at the corner of Lake Street and Hennepin Avenue. Expensive bistros, art-house cinemas, ethnic eateries and beer-and-burger bars all thrive in Uptown, along with small performance spaces and many coffeehouses. Although Uptown has endured the arrival of national clothing stores and strip malls, small, eccentric businesses still thrive there. The recording artist sometimes known as Prince has a boutique on Lake Street. On the first weekend in August, Uptown hosts the country's largest outdoor art fair along Hennepin Avenue.

Rents in Uptown are moderate, although apartments closest to Lake and Hennepin can be much more expensive. This is also the most racially mixed area of Calhoun-Isles, with substantial numbers of African-American, Asian, and Native American residents. Sturdy Midwestern-square style houses predominate, mixed with stately brick apartment buildings. Much of the housing in Uptown dates to the first quarter of the century or earlier, but it is regularly interspersed with modular low-rise apartment complexes built in the 1960s and 70s.

There's a lot to do here! You can take in a movie at the Lagoon or a production at the Jungle Theater, then talk over wine or a latté at a streetside cafe and stroll home amid the traffic madness. Of course, the madness is with you to stay if you live in these neighborhoods. Parking can be a hassle, and residents have to protect against car theft.

Bryn Mawr, Cedar-Isles-Dean, West Calhoun

These neighborhoods contain moderately priced, single-family homes close to the lakes. The stucco bungalows and turn of the century wood-frame houses offer comfortable living with large tree-shaded yards. In Cedar-Isles-Dean and West Calhoun there are also high-rise apartment buildings along Excelsior Boulevard with lake views. When the weather gets warm, the parkways adjoining Lake Calhoun and Lake of the Isles are literally swarming with runners, bikers and cars. Bryn Mawr does not experience as much of a migration, although it is adjacent to Cedar Lake and the Wirth Park Woods.

Kenwood

Encircling Lake of the Isles, Kenwood is perhaps the most affluent neighborhood in Minneapolis. Large, well-manicured lawns, security systems and wrought iron fences sweep up from the public parkways. The neighborhood's hills are graced with numerous Colonials, Arts and Crafts and Mediterranean style homes, as well as a few contemporary designs that defy description. Most of these houses are architecturally striking and well worth a walk around the lake.

No matter where you live in Calhoun-Isles, the lakes are nearby, and people use them year-round. The Wirth Park Woods that abut the northern edge of Bryn Mawr are connected to Cedar Lake, Lake of the Isles, and Lake Calhoun by paved trails and parkways. The trail system is described in more detail in the chapter **Lakes and Parkways**.

Area Code: 612

Zip Codes: 55403, 55405, 55408, 55409, 55416

Post Offices: Loring Station, 18 North 12th St. Lake St. Station, 10 East 31st Street. Elmwood Branch, 3532 Beltline Blvd., St. Louis Park. (All post office branches can be reached at 349-4711.)

Police Precinct: 5th, 2429 Nicollet Ave., 673-5705.

Emergency Hospitals: Hennepin County Medical Center, 701 Park Ave., 347-2121. Methodist Hospital, 6500 Excelsior Blvd., St. Louis Park, 932-5000.

Library: Walker, 2880 Hennepin Ave., 823-8688.

Bus Lines: 1: Apache Plaza/Kenwood/Downtown. **4:** Southtown/Lyndale Ave./Downtown. **6:** Southdale/Hennepin Ave./Rosedale. **8:** St. Louis Park/Bryn Mawr/Downtown. **9:** Golden Valley/Glenwood Ave./Downtown. **17:** Knollwood Shopping Center/Hennepin Ave./Nicollet Mall. **21:** Lake St./Marshall Ave. (St. Paul). **23:** 38th St./Lake St./Becketwood. **59:** St. Louis Park/I-394 Frontage Rd./Downtown. **94L:** Lake St./I-94/Downtown St. Paul.

Neighborhood Organizations:
Bryn Mawr Neighborhood Association, 377-4634.
Calhoun Area Residents Action Group (CARAG), 823-2520.
Cedar-Isles-Dean Neighborhood Association, 832-3806.
East Calhoun Community Organization (ECCO), 822-8899.
East Isles Residents Association, 871-1528.
Kenwood Isles Area Association, 377-5572.
Lowry Hill Residents, Inc., 377-5346.
Lowry Hill East Neighborhood Association, 377-1561.
West Calhoun Neighborhood Council, 928-3511.

Southwest

Armatage	Fulton	Linden Hills
East Harriet	Kenny	Lynnhurst
Fuller	King Field	Windom

Boundaries: North: 38th St., **West:** France Ave., Xerxes Ave., **South:** Cross-town Highway 62. **East:** I-35W.

The quiet, tree-lined streets and staid, well-kept yards of the Southwest community make you feel as if you're in a much smaller city than you are. No more than ten minutes' drive from the high-rises of downtown, this is the most heavily residential area of Minneapolis.

Single-family homes and duplexes predominate, although apartments are available, especially in the Windom neighborhood. Most homes date to the early 1900s through the 1940s. Colonials and Midwestern squares line central streets such as Lyndale Avenue, while stucco bungalows are common toward the outer edges of the community. Homes surrounding Lake Harriet and the Lake Harriet Rock Garden are expensive, but moderately-priced ideal starter homes abound elsewhere. "Tangletown," inside the Fuller neighborhood to the southeast, is a hilly tangle of curved streets that are unusual in the mostly grid-like South Minneapolis layout. About ten percent of the residents in King Field and Windom are African-American, and many Lao, Filipino, and Vietnamese live in the area.

Numerous parks add to the tranquillity of the community. Lake Harriet is encircled by a parkway, and a bandshell on its north shore stages music in the summer. Martin Luther King Park to the northeast has indoor tennis courts. Lyndale Farmstead was the original home of Theodore Wirth, the turn-of-the-century "father" of Minneapolis parks. It features after-school programs, films, and an ice skating rink. The Minnehaha Creek Parkway runs through the community to the south.

Linden Hills

Once the location of resorts tucked in between Lakes Harriet and Calhoun, Linden Hills offers a pleasant assortment of tree-shaded homes, shops, restaurants and a food co-op on the side of a rolling slope. Bungalows predominate, but are intermixed with Colonials and some Prairie style houses. Property values are moderate to high. The commercial district of Linden Hills brings to mind the Main Streets of the small tourist towns on the St. Croix River just east of the Twin Cities. There are several unique galleries and shops, and many older storefronts. Best of all, it's quiet—a tranquil haven in the middle of the city.

Area Code: 612

Zip Codes: 55409, 55410, 55419

Post Offices: Lake St. Station, 110 East 31st St. Edina Branch, 3948 West 49 1/2 St., Edina. Diamond Lake Station, 5500 Nicollet Ave. (All post office branches can be reached at 349-4711.)

Police Precinct: 5th, 2429 Nicollet Ave., 673-5705.

Emergency Hospitals: Fairview Southdale Hospital, 6401 France Ave. South, 924-5000. Abbott Northwestern Hospital, 800 East 28th St., 863-4000.

Libraries: Linden Hills, 2900 West 43rd St., 922-2600. Washburn, 4747 Nicollet Ave., 825-4863.

Bus Lines: 4: Downtown/Bryant Ave./Southtown. **6:** Downtown/Windom neighborhood/Bloomington. **28:** Downtown/Xerxes Ave./Southdale. Numerous 35 routes run through southwestern neighborhoods onto I-35W. **47:** Downtown/Lyndale Ave./Normandale Community College. **68:** Cross-town Hwy 62/I-35W.

Neighborhood Organizations:
Armatage Neighborhood Association, 649-4501.
East Harriet-Farmstead, 824-9350.
Tangletown Neighborhood Association (Fuller), 823-5984.
Fulton Neighborhood Association, 922-3106.
Kenny Neighborhood Association, 827-9438.
Kingfield Neighborhood Association, 379-5980.
Linden Hills Neighborhood Council, 920-3572.
Lynnhurst Neighborhood Association, 823-5190.
Windom Community Council, 869-8522.

Nokomis

Diamond Lake	Keewaydin	Page
Ericsson	Minnehaha	Regina
Field	Morris Park	Wenonah
Hale	Northrup	

Boundaries: North: 42nd St., Hiawatha Golf Course. **West:** I-35W. **South:** Cross-town Highway 62. **East:** Hiawatha Ave., 47th Avenue.

In many ways, this region looks like the Southwest community, with tree-lined blocks of pleasant yards and tidy houses. However, Nokomis is more moderately priced and more recently developed, with homes largely built since the 1930s. The heart of the community, Lake Nokomis, is an expansive body of water with more green space around it than the other lakes of South Minneapolis. Small commercial districts are found throughout the area.

The Nokomis community is over eighty percent single-family homes, the city's highest concentration. Some luxurious Colonials line the curved parkways around Lake Nokomis; otherwise, there are many bungalows and Tudors, and occasionally, one-story ranch houses. Brick apartment buildings dating to the 1920s can be found along larger streets such as Chicago Avenue and Cedar Avenue near Lake Nokomis. Most of Nokomis is white, although over half of the residents in the Regina neighborhood are African-American.

Noise from Minneapolis/St. Paul International Airport, to the southeast, is a factor to consider if you're looking at Nokomis. The sound of jet engines taking off and landing particularly affects the Morris Park and Wenonah neighborhoods in the far-southeast corner of the city, but it's apparent elsewhere. Northwest Airlines, a hub carrier at the airport, is phasing out its loud, old 727s and DC-9s, which may reduce the noise disturbance. Also, the city offers federal grants for household sound insulation, a remedy many Nokomis residents reportedly have taken with success.

The city's venerable lake-parkway system winds through this community along Minnehaha Creek and around Lake Nokomis, leading to the public Hiawatha Golf Course and Lake Hiawatha. Baseball fields, open space and sparse wooded areas surround Lake Nokomis. Bring a picnic lunch, tour around by bicycle, or put down a blanket and read.

Area Code: 612

Zip Codes: 55406, 55407, 55409, 55417, 55419

Post Offices: Nokomis Station, 5139 34th Ave. South. Diamond Lake Station, 5500 Nicollet Ave. (All post office branches can be reached at 349-4711.)

Police Precinct: 3rd, 3000 Minnehaha Ave., 673-5703.

Emergency Hospitals: Abbott Northwestern Hospital, 800 East 28th St., 863-4000.

Library: Nokomis, 5100 34th Ave. South, 729-5989.

Bus Lines: 5: Downtown/Chicago Ave./Mall of America. **7**: Downtown/Minnehaha Ave./International Airport. **14**: Bloomington Ave./Downtown/Brooklyn Park. **15**: Southdale/Hiawatha Ave./Ford Pkwy. (St. Paul). **19**: 28th Ave. S./Downtown/Golden Valley. **22**: 34th Ave./42nd St./Cedar Ave.

Neighborhood Organizations:
Hale Page Diamond Lake Community Association, 824-7707.
Field Regina Northrup Neighborhood Group, 721-5424.
Nokomis East Neighborhood Group, 724-5652.
Standish-Ericsson Neighborhood Association, 721-1601.

Powderhorn

Bancroft	Corcoran	Standish
Bryant	Lyndale	Whittier
Central	Powderhorn Park	

Boundaries: North: Franklin Ave., Lake St., **West:** Lyndale Ave., I-35W. **South:** 38th St., 42nd Street. **East:** Minnehaha Ave.

When the snow begins to fall, the rolling hills of Powderhorn Park become a well-used tobogganing area. The community centers around the park, a square-mile reserve of hilly woods with a small lake set aside in the 1890s. The lake lost its crescent "powderhorn" shape when city planners dredged a marsh adjacent to it, but it's still a welcome expanse amid its urban surroundings.

Diversity is what the Powderhorn community is all about; diversity in income, ethnicity, housing type, and lifestyle. There are artists, older residents tending gardens, professionals, and blue-collar workers. On the first weekend in May everyone comes out for a rollicking "pagan" spring parade, staged by the Heart of the Beast Puppet Theater, which winds up with a day-long festival at the park.

As in much of the central city, Midwestern square style houses and stately brick apartments from the first quarter of the century are the main architectural features. In Powderhorn they are interspersed with large old Colonials and Victorian houses on wide lots. These grand houses, some of the oldest homes in Minneapolis, are prevalent along Blaisdell and Third Avenues near the Minneapolis Institute of Arts.

The duplexes and apartments in Whittier and Lyndale to the west are much like nearby neighborhoods in Uptown, although housing here is generally more affordable and incomes are more modest. Many different groups live together here: residents in Whittier and Lyndale are younger and less affluent; Standish in the southeast corner has older, wealthier residents. Bryant and Central are substantially African-American, and Native American, Lao, Hmong, and Latino residents live throughout the area. Home and car security may be an issue for those considering living in Powderhorn.

Restaurants, shops and cafes at the corner of Lake Street and Lyndale Avenue mark the beginnings of Uptown. Heading east from Lyndale, Lake Street is a thriving old-style commercial district, with diners, drugstores, and thrift stores. Plans are in the works for a large shopping development on the current site of the massive art-deco Sears building on Lake Street. Also on Lake Street is the Heart of the Beast Puppet Theater (the venue that produces the May Day parade), where theatrical productions and workshops take place throughout the year. Would-be residents seeking peace and quiet may find eastern Lake Street a bit rambunctious at night.

Area Code: 612

Zip Codes: 55405, 55406, 55407, 55408, 55409

Post Offices: Powderhorn Station, 3045 Bloomington Ave., Minnehaha Station, 3033 27th Ave. South. Lake St. Station, 110 East 31st St. (All post office branches can be reached at 349-4711.)

Police Precincts: West of I-35W: 5th, 2429 Nicollet Ave., 673-5705. Rest of Powderhorn: 3rd, 3000 Minnehaha Ave., 673-5703.

Emergency Hospital: Abbott Northwestern Hospital, 800 East 28th St., 863-4000.

Library: Hosmer, 347 East 36th St., 824-4848.

Bus Lines: 4: Downtown/Lyndale Ave./Southtown. **5:** Downtown/Chicago Ave./Mall of America. **9:** 4th Ave./ Downtown/Golden Valley. **10:** Grand Ave./Downtown/northeast Minneapolis. **14:** Bloomington Ave./Downtown/Brooklyn Park. **18**: Downtown/Nicollet Ave./Bloomington. **19:** Mall of America/Cedar Ave./Downtown. **21:** Lake St. **22:** Cedar Ave./Downtown. **23:** 38th St. **47:** Downtown/Lyndale Ave./Normandale Community College. **94L:** Lake St./I-94/ Downtown St. Paul. Numerous I-35W routes board where the highway crosses Lake Street.

Neighborhood Organizations:
Bancroft Neighborhood Association, 724-5313.
Bryant Neighborhood Organization, 824-3453.
Central Neighborhood Improvement Association, 822-3302.
Corcoran Neighborhood Association, 724-7457.
Lyndale Neighborhood Association, 824-9402.
Powderhorn Park Neighborhood Association, 722-4817.
Standish-Ericsson Neighborhood Association, 721-1601.
Whittier Alliance, 871-7756.

Phillips

Boundaries: North: I-94. **West:** I-35W. **South:** Lake St. **East:** Hiawatha Ave.

The Phillips community in south-central Minneapolis has a complex history. Elegant Victorian mansions, some of the largest in the city, are a sign of past grandeur. Unfortunately, recent deterioration, due in part to construction of Interstate Highways 35W and 94, has laid many of these stately houses to waste. In contrast, community activism has led to a few shining examples of urban renewal and rehabilitation. The community's sense of pride is exemplified by a graceful gateway sculpture at Franklin and Chicago Avenues built by Rafala Green.

Some of the sturdy 19th-century rowhouses and massive Victorian homes along Franklin and Chicago Avenues have been converted into apartments and office spaces. Buildings have also been adapted for use by the cluster of hospitals and specialty clinics in Phillips, including Abbott Northwestern Hospital and Minneapolis Children's Medical Center. Perhaps the neighborhood's best-known landmark is the American Swedish Institute, a 33-room mansion that houses a museum of Swedish culture at 2600 Park Ave.

Almost a quarter of Phillips residents are Native American, making it the urban center for Native Americans in the Midwest, if not the nation. The Minneapolis American Indian Center (with a gallery) is at the corner of Franklin and Bloomington Avenues, and Little Earth of United Tribes, a large Native American apartment complex, is on Cedar Avenue at 25th Street. African-American residents make up about a fifth of the neighborhood. Phillips is also home to many recent émigrés from Ethiopia, and north African restaurants and food stores can be found a little north of the neighborhood on Cedar Avenue.

Revitalization projects continue to bring new capital into Phillips. East Lake Street may soon see a comprehensive rehab, centered around a new mall on the site of the old Sears building at 10th Avenue. Still, Phillips is an urban neighborhood in transition, and newcomers should be aware of this when considering living here.

Area Code: 612

Zip Codes: 55403, 55404, 55405, 55407, 55408

Post Offices: Powderhorn Station, 3045 Bloomington Ave., Minnehaha Station, 3033 27th Ave. South. Lake St. Station, 110 East 31st St. (All post office branches can be reached at 349-4711.)

Police Precinct: 3rd, 3000 Minnehaha Ave., 673-5703.

Emergency Hospital: Abbott Northwestern Hospital, 800 East 28th St., 863-4000.
Library: Franklin, 1314 East Franklin Ave., 874-1667.

Bus Lines: 2: Franklin Ave./U. of M. **5:** Downtown/Chicago Ave./Mall of America. **9:** 4th Ave./Downtown/Golden Valley. **14:** Bloomington Ave./Downtown/Brooklyn Park. **19:** Mall of America/Cedar Ave./Golden Valley. **21:** Lake St. **22:** Cedar Ave./Park Ave. **94L:** Lake St./I-94. Numerous I-35W express routes board where the highway crosses Lake Street.

Neighborhood Organization:
People of Phillips, 874-1711.

Longfellow

Cooper	Howe
Hiawatha	Seward

Boundaries: **North**: I-94. **West**: Minnehaha Ave. **South/East**: Mississippi River.

Longfellow is the sliver-shaped region of south-eastern Minneapolis that flanks the gorge of the Mississippi River, and includes Minnehaha Falls Park. Residents of Longfellow have easy access to nature walks. Minnehaha Falls Park is composed of several square miles of woods and bluffs around the gorge where Minnehaha Creek empties into the Mississippi River. Trails in the park connect to the lake parkway system, so you could ride your bike from here for several miles and never encounter city streets.

This pleasant community was developed more recently than most of south Minneapolis: rows of modest homes with big backyards are suggestive of inner-ring suburbs. Affordable 1940s-era bungalows and Tudor homes set into the flat plain above the Mississippi make up the southern four neighborhoods of Longfellow. Larger, tree-shaded Colonials can be seen along Mississippi River Boulevard. This is quintessential family living: middle class, tidy yards, and plenty of parks.

Seward

The northern wedge of Longfellow, the Seward neighborhood has a mix of residents—young and old, artists and professionals. Houses here are Longfellow's most affordable and, by their proximity to the earliest settlements in the center of the city, also Longfellow's oldest. Victorian and Midwestern square houses are mixed in with occasional small brick workers' cottages over a hundred years old. You'll notice interesting paint jobs on some of the 19th century homes and a number of unconventional gardens—all part of the offbeat, organic style of Seward. East Franklin Avenue is dotted with small businesses, cafes and a food co-op. The University of Minnesota is easily accessible, just to the north across the Mississippi River.

Area Code: 612

Zip Codes: 55404, 55406, 55407, 55417

Post Offices: Minnehaha Station, 3033 27th Ave. South. Nokomis Station, 5139 34th Ave. South. (All post office branches can be reached at 349-4711.)

Police Precinct: 3rd, 3000 Minnehaha Ave., 673-5703.

Emergency Hospitals: Abbott Northwestern Hospital, 800 East 28th St., 863-4000. Fairview Riverside Medical Center, 2450 Riverside Avenue, 672-6000.

Library: East Lake, 2727 East Lake St., 724-4561.

Bus Lines: 2: Franklin Ave./U. of M. **7:** Downtown/Minnehaha Ave./Mall of America. **8:** Franklin Ave./Downtown/Golden Valley. **15:** Southdale/54th St./Ford Pkwy.(St. Paul). **20:** 46th Ave./Plymouth Ave. **21:** Lake St. **23:** 46th Ave./38th St.

Neighborhood Organizations:
Longfellow Community Council, 722-4529.
Seward Neighborhood Group, 338-6205.

University

Cedar-Riverside (West Bank)	Nicollet Island (East Bank)
Como	Prospect Park
Marcy-Holmes	University of Minnesota

Boundaries: North: East Hennepin Ave., I-35W. **West:** Nicollet Island, I-35W. **South:** I-94, East Bank of Mississippi. **East:** city limits.

A diverse mix of neighborhoods is tucked in along the banks of the Mississippi with direct access to the University of Minnesota's massive campus. Housing ranges from the multitudes of student apartments next to campus to the low-rent high-rises at Cedar-Riverside to older neighborhoods in Prospect Park and Como. Due to the campus location, rents are not a bargain, although house prices are moderate.

The perks of a university—lectures, concerts, the University Film Society—are easily accessible to people living in these neighborhoods. Dinkytown, the main campus commercial district, has plenty of cheap places to eat and many businesses named "Gopher" (you guessed it: the University of Minnesota mascot). Dinkytown is located between Southeast Eighth Street and University Avenue just northwest of the U of M campus.

Buildings from the city's earliest settlement still stand in the Nicollet Island neighborhood, northwest of the U of M campus. The St. Anthony Main commercial plaza is rehabbed from the brick and stone storefronts of the original Main Street of St. Anthony, the municipal predecessor to Minneapolis. The Nicollet Island neighborhood is a mix of residential areas and commercial corners. To the east, the Como neighborhood is a swath of modest bungalow homes populated by manufacturing workers and people connected to the university, including students.

Cedar-Riverside

Across the river on the West Bank, the Cedar-Riverside neighborhood (named for the crossing of the two streets) has more of an urban feel. In the 1960s, Cedar-Riverside became a center for alternative culture. A creative element is still evident here in the many music (particularly blues) venues, small performance theaters, and cooperatively-run vegetarian restaurants. Ethiopian, Indian, and Cuban restaurants thrive in the neighborhood. The Riverside Plaza, a low-rent high-rise whose colored squares are visible from I-94, looms above the neighborhood. A residential area, including Midwestern square-style duplexes and apartments, lies to the east of Cedar Avenue. Newcomers should be aware that security is a concern in the streets of Cedar-Riverside.

Prospect Park

The "witch's hat" roof of the Prospect Park stone water tower is clearly visible from I-94. Stately, older Tudor and Colonial-style homes stand on the steep slopes below the tower, although cheaper apartments are available. Many University faculty and students live here, and a sizable number of residents are Hmong-and Chinese-Americans. A lower-income section including public housing is on Prospect Park's western edge. An active neighborhood organization, quiet streets and tree-covered slopes give the neighborhood a tranquil character.

Area Code: 612

Zip Codes: 55455 (University of Minnesota), 55413, 55414, 55454, 55404

Post Offices: University Station, 2811 University Ave. SE. Dinkytown Station, 1311 SE 4th St. (All post office branches can be reached at 349-4711.)

Police Precinct: 2nd, 1911 Central Ave. NE, 673-5702.

Emergency Hospitals: University of Minnesota Hospital, Harvard St. at East River Parkway, 626-3000. Fairview Riverside Medical Center, 2450 Riverside Ave., 672-6000.

Library: Southeast, 1222 SE 4th Street, 378-1816. University libraries, administrative offices: 624-4520.

Bus Lines: 1: Kenwood/East Hennepin Ave./Apache Plaza. **2:** Franklin Ave./U of M **6:** Southdale/U of M/Rosedale. **16:** Downtown/University Ave. **33:** Downtown/East Hennepin Ave./Arden Hills. **95:** U of M/Downtown St. Paul. **105:** University Ave./U of M St. Paul Campus. The U of M 52 routes run from many parts of the Twin Cities to campus on weekdays. Call 625-9000.

Neighborhood Organizations:
Cedar-Riverside Project Area Committee, 338-6375.
Marcy-Holmes Neighborhood Association, 379-3814.
Nicollet Island PAC, 340-7934.
Prospect Park East River Road Improvement Association, 331-2970.

Northeast

Audubon Park	Holland	St. Anthony West, East
Beltrami	Logan Park	Sheridan
Bottineau	Marshall Terrace	Waite Park
Columbia Park	Northeast Park	Windom Park

Boundaries: North: 37th Ave., NE. **West:** Mississippi River. **South:** Nicollet Island, Central Ave., I-35W. **East:** city limits.

Two blocks after crossing the river on Hennepin Avenue, the large storefront of Kramarczuk's East European Deli ushers you into the city's old working-class neighborhood. Heading north along Central Avenue, you'll see more delis, polka lounges and supper clubs, as well as rows of small, affordable Midwestern square houses and bungalows. The Northeast community is made up largely of residents of German,

Swedish, Norwegian, Polish, and Ukrainian backgrounds. "Nord'east," as residents call it, isn't all polkas, however; a few good Mediterranean bakeries and delis are on Central, and a number of Native American and Asian residents live in neighborhoods closer to the University.

Rents are quite affordable in the southern neighborhoods close to the U of M campus; Midwestern squares and small turn-of-the-century wood frame houses predominate. The four "Park" neighborhoods (Waite, Audubon, Windom and Northeast) to the north, however, have more in common with the suburbs they adjoin, than with the rest of the neighborhoods in the Northeast. Incomes are higher in these newer neighborhoods.

A stretch of parkway runs from Hillside Cemetery through the community along St. Anthony Boulevard, and reaches the Mississippi River to the north. There are also many small parks to visit with your kids, unwind, or walk the dog.

Area Code: 612

Zip Codes: 55413, 55418

Post Office: East Side Station, 1600 18th Ave. NE. (All post office branches can be reached at 349-4711.)

Police Precinct: 2nd, 1911 Central Ave. NE, 673-5702.

Emergency Hospital: University of Minnesota Hospital, Harvard St. at East River Parkway, 626-3000.

Libraries: Northeast, 2200 Central Ave. NE, 789-1800.
Pierre Bottineau, 1224 Second St. NE, 379-2609.

Bus Lines: 1: Kenwood/East Hennepin Ave./Apache Plaza. **4:** Downtown/Johnson St. NE/New Brighton. **10:** South Minneapolis/Central Ave./New Brighton. **11:** Lowry Ave. NE/Rosedale. **18:** 2nd St. NE/western neighborhoods. **24:** Downtown/University Ave. NE/Coon Rapids. **25:** Downtown/Johnson St. NE/Northtown. **27:** Downtown/Marshall St./Anoka. **29:** Downtown/Marshall Ave./Blaine. Numerous routes take I-35W to northern and eastern suburbs.

Neighborhood Organizations:
Audubon Neighborhood Association, 788-8790.
Beltrami Neighborhood Council, 331-7839.
Bottineau Neighborhood Association, 782-2145.
Columbia Park Neighborhood Association, 489-8288.
Holland Neighborhood Improvement Association, 781-2299.
Logan Park Neighborhood Association, 781-0700.
Northeast Park Neighborhood Association, 781-6620.

St. Anthony East Neighborhood Association, 379-9381.
St. Anthony West Neighborhood Association, 378-8886.
Sheridan Today and Yesterday, 627-9120.
Waite Park Community Council, 788-4040.
Windom Park Community, 781-1307.

Camden

Cleveland	McKinley
Folwell	Shingle Creek
Lind-Bohanon	Victory

Boundaries: North: 53rd Ave., North. **West:** Xerxes Ave., North. **South:** Lowry Ave., North. **East:** Mississippi River.

Camden is located in the northernmost part of the city, west of the Mississippi River. It is comprised of industrial zones and middle-to-lower income working-class areas. Almost eighty percent of the houses in Camden are single-unit homes, primarily two-story woodframes and bungalows.

Homes are slightly more expensive and incomes are slightly higher in the Victory area, although all of the neighborhoods are modest in comparison to the rest of Minneapolis. The Camden community is predominantly white, but a variety of racial and ethnic groups are scattered throughout, including African Americans, Native Americans and Latino Americans.

There's no shortage of places to walk or ride your bike in Camden. At Webber Park you can wander along a narrow swath of park land that follows the Mississippi as far north as the city limits. The city's parkway system picks up here from the northeast side of town and continues along Memorial Parkway, then turns south along the city's western boundary. From here, you could bike your way as far south as Minnehaha Falls State Park.

Area Code: 612

Zip Codes: 55412, 55430

Post Offices: Lowry Ave. Station, 2306 Lowry Ave. North.
(All post office branches can be reached at 349-4711.)

Police Precinct: 4th, 1925 Plymouth Ave. North, 673-5704.

Emergency Hospital: North Memorial Medical Center,
3300 Oakdale Ave. North, Robbinsdale, 520-5200.

Library: Webber Park, 4310 Webber Parkway, 522-3182.

Bus Lines: 5: Downtown/Lowry Ave. N/Brooklyn Center.
7: Lowry Ave. N/Downtown/Mall of America. **11:** Lowry Ave.
N/Rosedale. **22:** Downtown/Lyndale Ave. N/Brooklyn Park.
81: Downtown/Fremont Ave./Hennepin Tech. **84:** Downtown/Fre-
mont Ave./Brooklyn Center. Numerous 94 Express buses enter I-94
at 49th Avenue N.

Neighborhood Organizations:
Cleveland Neighborhood Association, 522-8167.
Folwell Neighborhood Revitalization Committee, 331-1448.
Lind-Bohanon Neighborhood Association, 588-7641.
McKinley Neighborhood Association, 522-7989.
Shingle Creek Neighborhood Association, 781-1191.
Victory Neighborhood Association, 529-9558.

Near North

Harrison   Sumner-Glenwood
Hawthorne   Willard-Hay
Jordan

Boundaries: North: Lowry Ave. **West:** Xerxes Ave. **South:** Bassett
Creek. **East:** I-94, Mississippi River.

The Near North community is a modest district of older homes, apartments and family businesses. The characteristic shared by most residents throughout Near North is a median household income that ranks
among the lowest in the city. But with its community outreach programs,
incluing the North Side Residents Redevelopment Council which sponsors youth mentoring programs, internships and other community-build-
ing initiatives, as well as the numerous cultural organizations, businesses, and entertainment venues here, there is a strong community spirit in
this ethnically diverse neighborhood. More than half of the residents of
Near North are African American. The area is also home to many Asian
and Native Americans. The clubs of Near North offer an interesting variety of music: from rythym and blues to country to big band crooning, you
can hear it all in this neighborhood.
    Almost half of the homes in the area are single-unit, with the remainder
split between duplexes and apartments. Many residents work in service or
manufacturing occupations, although professionals, living in more palatial
residences, can be found in Willard-Hay to the west. An expansive public
housing project makes up much of Sumner-Glenwood. The Harrison neighborhood just north of Bassett Creek has become a popular area for rehabs
due in part to its convenience to Downtown (the Minneapolis Community
Development Agency offers below-market fix-up loans to people with lower
incomes for just this purpose). Note: security, particularly for those unfamil-
iar with the area, can be a concern in some parts of the Near North.

Area Code: 612

Zip Codes: 55405, 55411

Post Offices: Loring Station, 18 North 12th St. Lowry Ave. Station, 2306 Lowry Ave. North. (All post office branches can be reached at 349-4711.)

Police Precinct: 4th, 1925 Plymouth Ave. North, 673-5704.

Emergency Hospitals: North Memorial Medical Center, 3300 Oakdale Ave. North, Robbinsdale, 520-5200. Hennepin County Medical Center, 701 Park Ave., 347-2121.
Libraries: North Regional, 1315 Lowry Ave. North, 522-3333. Sumner, 611 Emerson Ave. North, 374-5642.

Bus Lines: 5: Downtown/Fremont Ave. N/Brooklyn Center. **7:** Lowry Ave./Downtown/Mall of America. **14:** Downtown/Broadway/Brooklyn Park. **19:** Mall of America/Downtown/Golden Valley. **20:** Plymouth Ave./Cedar-Riverside/Highland (St. Paul). **22:** Downtown/Lyndale Ave. N/Brooklyn Park. **55:** State Hwy 55. Numerous express lines board at stops along I-94.

Neighborhood Organizations:
Harrison Neighborhood Association, 374-4849.
Hawthorne Area Community Council, 529-6033.
Jordan Area Community Council, 521-8436.
Northside Residents Redevelopment Council, 335-5924.
Sumner-Olson Resident Council, 342-1523.

St. Paul

With an official population of 271,660 (1994), St. Paul is stuck with being known as The Other City. If you visit St. Paul, you may get the impression that it's an older city, although that's barely true. St. Paul was settled slightly earlier than Minneapolis, but what makes St. Paul seem older is the fact that much more of the early city still survives—older buildings, narrower streets, divided boulevards. From Governor Alexander Ramsey's beautiful house Downtown built between 1868-1872, to sumptuously ornamental Summit Hill, much of St. Paul still possesses a stately 19th century elegance.

The following pages describe St. Paul's seventeen neighborhood districts, each with its own character and history. The streets of St. Paul are thought to be quieter and more wholly residential than in Minneapolis. You can make your own judgment on that. What is clear is that people in St. Paul are proud of their neighborhoods. Neighborhood organizations (called district councils here) are the places to call if you want more information on a specific neighborhood. The district councils work together with city government to keep life in St. Paul as tranquil as it is reputed to be.

A note about the St. Paul police system: the police are split into three patrol teams, western (north and south), central and eastern. The telephone numbers given are for the stations where officers prepare to go out on patrol. You can also talk to the St. Paul Central Police Office, at 291-1111. Of course, in any emergency, call 911.

Downtown

Boundaries: North: University Ave. **West:** Marion St., Irvine Ave. **South:** Kellogg Blvd., Mississippi River. **East:** I-94, Lafayette Rd.

One hundred and fifty years ago, when St. Paul played a major role in the river trade, the streets of what is today downtown, bustled with activity. Boats carrying commercial cargo and people to and from St. Paul swarmed the upper Mississippi. The river established St. Paul as an economic power in the early Midwest. Today there's not much left of that early hubbub on the Mississippi, although you can still watch cargo barges make their way through downtown from bridges high above. The river's low profile may change, though, after completion of a few city projects at the water's edge. The Science Museum of Minnesota is slated to be moved to the river's northern bluff, with descending steps that promise to provide a spectacular view. Also, Harriet Island, which had a public bath house and zoo at the turn of the century, is expected to receive a National Park System visitor center.

Downtown is dotted with high-rise apartment buildings, containing moderate rent apartments and some luxury suites. The State Capitol building and state offices are here, as are headquarters for a few large companies. Although signs of life diminish dramatically when professionals and state workers leave in the early evening, today's Downtown is more versatile and culturally rich than it was thirty years ago. In the 1970s developers completed several high-rise apartments and renovations, including an overhaul of Lowertown, on the east side of downtown, one of St. Paul's two early river landings. Many of Lowertown's massive old brick buildings have been converted into office space and apartments, including an artists' loft cooperative. The neighborhood features an excellent farmers' market from spring through fall.

Today people flock to events at the Civic Center, the Ordway and Fitzgerald Theaters, the Science Museum of Minnesota, the Children's Museum, the Minnesota Museum of Art and to numerous festivals throughout the year. The century old St. Paul Winter Carnival is a major Downtown event that takes place in January and includes an ice sculpture contest at Rice Park, sled races and parades. Despite these activities, the downtown is still remarkably peaceful, which makes it pleasant for those who live here.

Area Code: 612

Zip Codes: 55101, 55102

Post Offices: Main Office, 180 East Kellogg Blvd. Pioneer Station, 141 East 4th St., Uptown-Skyway, 415 West Wabasha St. Riverview Station, 292 Eva St. (All post office branches can be reached at 349-4711.)

Police: Central District Patrol Team, 292-3563.

Emergency Hospitals: St. Paul-Ramsey Medical Center, 640 Jackson St., 221-3456. HealthEast St. Joseph's Hospital, 69 West Exchange St., 232-3000.

Library: Central, 90 West 4th St., 292-6311.

Bus Lines: Numerous city bus lines run through downtown, and you can get around Downtown by bus on most major streets. Check a transit map (an MCTO transit store in the American National Bank building at 5th and Minnesota Streets gives them out) or call the MCTO at 373-3333. Also, the Capital City Trolley runs shuttles around Downtown; call 223-5600. **54 Express:** 6th St./International Airport/Mall of America. **94B, C, D Express:** 6th St./I-94/downtown Minneapolis.

Neighborhood Organization:
Capitol River Council, 445 Minnesota St., Suite 524, 221-0488.

Summit Hill

Boundaries: North: Summit Ave. **West:** Ayd Mill Rd. **South/East**: I-35E.

Overlooking Downtown and the Mississippi River Valley, the bluffs of Summit Hill epitomize the grandeur and wealth of industrial boom-era St. Paul. All of Summit Avenue is protected, either as a national or local His- toric District. Railroad baron James J. Hill built a red sandstone mansion at 240 Summit Avenue. F. Scott Fitzgerald was born in the neighbor- hood, and returned to write for a while in a stone rowhouse apartment at 599 Summit Avenue. The Minnesota Historical Society arranges tours of many of the houses and gardens on Summit Hill.
    Having said that, Summit Hill is more than a museum of the lavish excesses of the late 19th century. It is possible to find an apartment in Summit Hill, although vacancy rates here are the lowest in the city. House prices are among the city's highest; many going for well over $200,000. But the engine driving those numbers up is Summit Avenue itself; the area south of Grand Avenue is more modest, as are surround- ing neighborhoods. People from all walks of life reside here, including

educators and students from Macalester College or one of the numerous other colleges in the area. The neighborhood is 97 percent white.

Besides the profusion of swank historic buildings, a major perk of the Summit Hill neighborhood is its proximity to Grand Avenue. Driving to the top of the hill on the eastern end of Grand, one passes an extensive strip of storefronts, many of them a hundred years old. Grand Avenue has developed into one of the Twin Cities' most attractive commercial districts, with interesting restaurants, specialty stores, taverns and bookstores. Shop around, have a latté at a streetside table, and perhaps drive to the end of the street to the Mississippi gorge for a pleasant walk. Whether or not you move to Summit Hill, be sure to check out Grand Avenue.

Area Code: 612

Zip Codes: 55102, 55105

Post Offices: Main Office, 180 East Kellogg Blvd. Elway Station, 1715 West 7th St. (All post office branches can be reached at 349-4711.)

Police: Western District Patrol Team, North: 292-3512, South: 292-3549.

Emergency Hospital: United Hospital, 333 Smith Ave. North, 220-8000.

Libraries: Central, 90 West 4th Street, 292-6311. Lexington, 1080 University Ave. West, 292-6620.

Bus Lines: 3: Grand Ave./Downtown/3M Center. **10:** St. Clair Ave./ Downtown/Hillcrest Center. **17:** Dale St./Rosedale.

Neighborhood Organization:
Summit Hill Association, 860 St. Clair Avenue, 222-1222.

Highland

Boundaries: North: Randolph Ave. **West/South:** Mississippi River. **East:** I-35W, Homer St. from West 7th St. to Shepard Rd.

The rolling meadows of today's Highland community accommodated St. Paul's earliest suburbs. In the 1880s, developers established four small villages west of city limits at Lexington Parkway. At the time, the area was known as Reserve Township, and most of it was farms and cow pasture. Commuter trains ran routes to the new villages, which included Merriam Park, Macalester Park, Groveland, and Saint Anthony Park. Highland, the vast acreage descending to the confluence of the Mississippi and Minnesota Rivers, was the last to be developed.

As a result, Highland looks newer than Macalester-Groveland and the other neighborhoods nearby. The oldest houses are farmhouses. You'll find many 1930s to 1970s bungalows and ramblers built on tidy lots along the gradual slopes of Highland, with a handful of opulent contemporary design houses tucked into the bluff along Mississippi River Boulevard. Many houses in Highland go for over $100,000, but mixed in with them is more moderately priced housing, including apartment buildings to accommodate students at the College of St. Catherine and other nearby colleges. Although Highland is 94 percent white, it is also home to the city's greatest number of Vietnamese American residents. In addition, Highland is home to a well-established Jewish community, and there are Jewish schools, associations and retail businesses in the neighborhood. The stability and peacefulness of the area is reminiscent of a small town, and makes Highland a much sought-after location by home buyers.

Although streets are quiet, a bustling commercial district centered around Highland Village on the eastern end of Ford Parkway (named for the fortress-like Ford assembly plant at the end of the parkway) includes bookstores, department stores, a movie theater and a few places to get an inexpensive dinner. Also, the neighborhood is close to Grand Avenue, with its endless array of places to shop. (Read more about Grand Avenue in the descriptions of Summit Hill and Macalester-Groveland.)

The other major perk of living in Highland is its proximity to green space and wilderness areas. Highland Park is a hilly expanse with a municipal golf course, outdoor swimming pools and cross country ski trails. More on the wild side, Hidden Falls and Crosby Farm Regional Parks are adjacent to the southern end of Highland. Nearby is the confluence of the Mississippi and Minnesota Rivers, which includes Minnehaha Falls and Fort Snelling State Parks and the Minnesota River National Wildlife Refuge. All of these are superb waterfowl watching areas, and none of them are far from Highland.

Area Code: 612

Zip Code: 55116

Post Office: Elway Station, 1715 West 7th St. (All post office branches can be reached at 349-4711.)

Police: Western District Patrol Team, North: 292-3512, South: 292-3549.

Emergency Hospital: United Hospital, 333 Smith Ave. North, 220-8000.

Library: Highland Park, 1974 Ford Parkway, 292-6622.

Bus Lines: 4: Mall of America/Snelling Ave./Rosedale. **7:** Cleveland Ave./Downtown/Signal Hills. **9:** Ford Pkwy./Downtown/Maplewood. **10:** Ford Pkwy./Downtown/Hillcrest Center. **14:** Ford Plant/Randolph Ave./Downtown. **54 Express:** W. 7th St./Minneapolis-St. Paul International Airport/Mall of America. **94H:** Ford Pkwy./I-94W/ Downtown Minneapolis. **94J:** Snelling Ave./I-94W/Downtown Minneapolis.

Neighborhood Organization:
Highland Area Community Council, 1978 Ford Parkway, 298-5138.

Macalester-Groveland

Boundaries: North: Summit Ave. **West:** Mississippi River. **South:** Randolph Ave. **East:** Ayd Mill Rd.

In the 1880s a group of Macalester College trustees bought a farm in what was then Reserve Township, an expanse of meadow west of St. Paul. They gave the college 40 acres and divided the rest into lots, thus creating one of the first communities outside of old St. Paul. At the time, it was a short train commute into town. Today, Macalester-Groveland is an epicenter of St. Paul activity, bustling with academic and commercial energy. There are three other private colleges in the area: the College of St. Catherine, University of St. Thomas, and the St. Paul Seminary. Academic life pervades the neighborhood: bookstores hold readings, colleges hold public lectures and concerts, and clusters of students hang out at offbeat shops, restaurants and coffee houses on Grand Avenue. All of this combines to make Mac-Groveland one of the most popular Twin Cities neighborhoods for newcomers.

As is usually the case, desirability comes at a price. Rents and house prices here are among the highest in St. Paul, although with persistence and luck relatively affordable apartments can be found. The best time to look in Mac-Groveland is in late spring, when students move out and sublets and leases become available.

The history of Mac-Groveland has resulted in an interesting mixture of housing designs. On and near Grand Avenue, handsome two- to four-story brick apartments from the 1920s are intermixed with the brick storefronts of cafés and retail businesses. These buildings first appeared after the turn of the century as Grand Avenue emerged as St. Paul's most lively commercial district. The first single-occupancy houses in the neighborhood were built in the 1880s on spacious prairie lots, followed by newer houses as those lots were repeatedly subdivided. Architectural styles run the gamut, from 19th century Tudor-style cottages and meticulous Arts-and-Crafts bungalows to contemporary designs from the 1960s. Bordering the neighborhood to the north are the opulent 19th-century mansions of Summit Avenue (read more about this elegant boulevard in the description of Summit Hill). Residential streets in Macalester-Groveland are attractive and tranquil, lined with mature oak and maple trees, and the bluffs of the Mississippi are never far away.

Grand Avenue is a popular strip of specialty retail stores, restaurants, and interesting bistros. There are scores of places to eat, drink, and argue politics and religion along the length of the street, but a focus of the academic spirit of the Mac-Groveland neighborhood is the Hungry Mind Bookstore, just west of the Macalester campus. Hungry Mind holds regular readings, publishes a quarterly book review, and is adjacent to the Table of Contents, a small restaurant. Traffic on Grand is heavy, but slow enough to make living near the street tolerable.

If you're tired of shopping or just want to get away, the Mississippi River gorge lies at the western end of the neighborhood. Land adjacent to the St. Paul Seminary is relatively wild and quite picturesque. Miles of river walking or bike riding are accessible from Mac-Groveland by the river parkway. If you settle here, you'll thank Bishop Thomas Grace of St. Thomas University for preserving the natural habitat along the river.

Area Code: 612

Zip Code: 55105

Post Offices: Elway Station, 1715 West 7th St. (All post office branches can be reached at 349-4711.)

Police: Western District Patrol Team, North: 292-3512, South: 292-3549.

Emergency Hospital: United Hospital, 333 Smith Ave. North, 220-8000.

Library: Merriam Park, 1831 Marshall Ave., 292-6624.

Bus Lines: 3: Grand Ave./Downtown/3M Center. **4:** Mall of America/Snelling Ave./Rosedale. **7:** Cleveland Ave./Downtown/Signal Hills. **10:** Ford Pkwy./Downtown/Hillcrest Center. **14:** Ford Plant/Randolph Ave./Downtown. **19:** Snelling Ave./Eagan. **94H:** Ford Pkwy./I-94W/Downtown Minneapolis. **94J:** Snelling Ave./I-94W/Downtown Minneapolis.

Neighborhood Organization:
Macalester-Groveland Community Council, 320 S. Griggs St., 698-7973.

Merriam Park, Snelling-Hamline, Lexington-Hamline

Boundaries: North: I-94, Cleveland Ave., University Ave. **West**: city limits, Mississippi River. **South**: Summit Ave. **East**: Lexington Parkway.

Bordered by the magnificent gorge of the Mississippi to the west and by the stone mansions of Summit Avenue to the south, Merriam Park is conveniently located midway between downtown Minneapolis and St. Paul. The Snelling-Hamline and Lexington-Hamline neighborhoods make up Merriam Park's eastern half. Although it is in the center of urban activity today, once upon a time Merriam Park was one of the Twin Cities' first suburbs, located a couple of trolley stops outside of early St. Paul. Colonel John Merriam, who in the 1880s owned much of the neighborhood's bluff land, envisioned the creation of a rural village built on large estates separated by abundant park land. Merriam built himself a luxurious house and then sold lots to those who would agree to his requirement that homes built on this land cost at least $1,500—a formidable amount at the time.

Traces of Merriam Park's exclusive beginnings are still apparent along the Mississippi, where turn-of-the-century Tudor and Arts-and-Crafts houses line streets shaded by mature, graceful elms. The Town and Country Club, a private club with a golf course, sprawls along the river north of Marshall avenue. The air of grandeur is embellished by miles of walking paths and park land along the river's edge. Move away from the Mississippi bluffs, though, and you will find the affordable housing that today predominates in Merriam Park as well as adjoining Snelling-Hamline and Lexington-Hamline. Due to student populations of the University of St. Thomas, Macalaster, and other nearby campuses, a good selection of reasonably priced apartments, duplexes and brick fourplexes is available in this area. If you're in the market for a house, the bungalows and Midwestern squares that line most of the neighborhood's streets are affordable to a middle income home buyer. For the Twin Cities, Merriam Park's ethnic mix is diverse.

One of the nice things about living in Merriam Park is its central location. The University of Minnesota is just north on River Road and events at Macalaster College and other campuses in the area are never far away. Residents can easily walk to many of the restaurants, shops and conveniences of Grand Avenue to the south (for more of a description of Grand Avenue, see the chapter "Shopping for the Home"). The Midway Shopping Center, also nearby at University and Snelling Avenues, offers staple needs at discount stores and supermarkets.

If you move here, you'll be able to enjoy the open splendor of the Mississippi bluffs. A pleasant hike along the river begins at Merriam Park, goes south to the Ford Parkway bridge, then north to the Marshall Avenue bridge. Don't miss it in October to see a color extravaganza.

Area Code: 612

Zip Code: 55104

Post Office: Industrial Station, 1430 Concordia Ave.
(All post office branches can be reached at 349-4711.)

Police: Western District Patrol Team, North: 292-3512, South: 292-3549.

Emergency Hospital: Fairview Riverside Medical Center, 2450 Riverside Ave. (Mpls.), 672-6000.

Library: Merriam Park, 1831 Marshall Ave., 292-6624.

Bus Lines: 3: Cretin Ave./Downtown/3M Center. **4:** Mall of America/Snelling Ave./Rosedale. **7:** Cleveland Ave./Downtown/Signal Hills. **16:** University Ave. **21:** Lake St. (Minneapolis)/Marshall Ave./Downtown. **22:** Concordia College/University Ave./Midway Shopping Center.

Neighborhood Organizations:
Merriam Park Community Council (West), 2000 St. Anthony Ave., 645-6887.
Snelling-Hamline Community Council (Central), 1573 Selby Ave., #319, 644-1085.
Lexington-Hamline Community Council (East), 1160 Selby Ave., 645-3207.

St. Anthony Park

Boundaries: North: city limits. **West:** city limits. **South:** I-94, B.N. Railroad. **East:** Cleveland Ave., Snelling Ave.

North of Merriam Park, Saint Anthony Park borders the University of Minnesota's St. Paul campus and forms the city's northwestern corner. Rolling hills and mature trees offset a variety of sturdy brick apartments and stately, older houses. St. Anthony Park is directly west of the University neighborhoods in Minneapolis, and offers a pleasant, relatively quiet alternative to living closer to the U of M campus.

The many quiet, curved streets clustered with wood frame and brick houses and apartments belie the area's central-city location. The streets were laid out in the 1870s by landscape architect Horace Cleveland. Cleveland's idea was to build a community of large rural estates that adapt to the natural textures of the land, so the streets follow the rolling slopes of the area instead of cutting across them. This explains the meandering avenues and somewhat oddly-shaped parks and greenways to be found here.

Although St. Anthony Park still has some of the original tranquillity its designer sought, the city has long since risen up around the neighborhood. The Burlington Northern Railroad segments the neighborhood into northern and southern halves, and State Highway 280 cuts through the west side. Northern Saint Anthony Park is an affluent twist of wooded residential streets containing larger recent Colonials and variations on Midwestern-square style houses. University faculty as well as students make up a good number of residents here. Heading south on Raymond Avenue, you go under the railroad bridge and pass by a large warehouse district before entering southern Saint Anthony Park, a more modest area made up mostly of single-family homes. Bungalows and Midwestern-square style houses predominate here. A majority of the neighborhood's residents are white, however, there is a substantial (approximately nine percent) Asian American population here too.

Saint Anthony park has several small commercial districts containing numerous locally-owned businesses. Bookstores and specialty shops line Como Avenue next to the U of M campus. Raymond Avenue is the site of several small cafes and restaurants, as well as a grocery co-op.

Following the eastern "arm" of the neighborhood, Energy Park Drive is a mixed-use strip of development that went up in the 1980s and includes apartment complexes and office space. At the far eastern end of Energy Park Drive is Municipal Stadium, host to occasional outdoor concerts and home of the St. Paul Saints Northern League baseball team. Although the Saints are a minor league team, their games have become quite popular, partly because of wacky promotions such as free back rubs during games. The Saints have also gained a following because they play outdoors on real turf, so their games are a great night out during the floppy days of summer. The team's stadium is a sort of miniature Wrigley Field—small enough not to have a great impact on surrounding neighborhoods.

Area Code: 612

Zip Codes: 55104, 55108, 55114

Post Office: Industrial Station, 1430 Concordia Ave. (All post office branches can be reached at 349-4711.)

Police: Western District Patrol Team, North: 292-3512, South: 292-3549.

Emergency Hospital: University of Minnesota Hospital, Harvard St. at East River Parkway, 626-3000.

Library: St. Anthony Park, 2245 Como Ave., 292-6635.

Bus Lines: 4: Rosedale/ Snelling Ave./Mall of America. **5:** Como Ave./Downtown/Signal Hills. **6:** Southdale/Como Ave./Rosedale. **12:** Downtown/Larpenteur Ave./Stillwater. **16:** Downtown Minneapolis/University Ave./Downtown St. Paul. **95E:** Downtown Minneapolis/Energy Park Dr./Downtown St. Paul. **105:** Raymond Ave./U. of M. St. Paul campus/Rosedale. Certain U. of M. 52 routes run from many parts of the Twin Cities to the St. Paul campus on weekdays. Call 625-9000. A Park N' Ride lot is at Eustis and Como Avenues.

Neighborhood Organization:
St. Anthony Park Community Council, 890 Cromwell Ave., 292-7884.

Hamline-Midway

Boundaries: North: B.N. Railroad. **West:** Cleveland Ave. **South:** University Ave. **East:** Lexington Parkway.

Just east of Saint Anthony Park is a swath of moderate to low-priced houses adjacent to St. Paul's Midway, a commercial thoroughfare that follows University Avenue. The Midway is one of the Twin Cities' busiest retail corridors, luring hordes of customers to discount grocery and department stores and other venues. The western end of the Midway is an industrial area containing warehouses, processing plants, and some office buildings. The other center of activity in the neighborhood is Hamline University, a private college on Snelling Avenue.

University Avenue was an early route between the two Twin Cities—by horse-drawn carriage, then electric streetcar, then by car—so the Hamline-Midway neighborhood emerged as the cities grew. Two thirds of the housing stock here went up before 1940, as reflected in the many commercial buildings on University Avenue that have an early-20th-century art-deco elegance and economy of design. Residences are for the most part solidly middle-class, with many modest wood frame Midwestern-square houses lining the streets north of University. Hamline-Midway might be a good place to look for a starter home, both because of the modest housing prices and for the convenience of living exactly halfway between the downtowns of both Twin Cities.

Living next to a major commercial thoroughfare such as the Midway can be a convenience or nuisance, depending on your point of view. It's nice to be able to walk to a bakery or to a performance at Ginkgo Coffeehouse. Take comfort in this: the Midway frenzy is mostly a daytime phenomenon. There are scattered taverns on University, but this is not a nightlife hotspot, unless your idea of a night out is going to Rainbow Foods at midnight (which it is for a dedicated handful).

Area Code: 612

Zip Code: 55104

Post Office: Industrial Station, 1430 Concordia Ave. (All post office branches can be reached at 349-4711.)

Police: Western District Patrol Team, North: 292-3512, South: 292-3549.

Emergency Hospital: University of Minnesota Hospital, Harvard Street at East River Parkway, 626-3000.

Library: Hamline Branch, 1558 Minnehaha Ave. West, 292-6632.

Bus Lines: 4: Rosedale/Snelling Ave./Mall of America.
7: Minnehaha Ave./Downtown/Signal Hills. **19:** Snelling Ave./Eagan.
22: St. Anthony Ave./Downtown/St. Paul-Ramsey Medical Center.

Neighborhood Organization:
Hamline-Midway Coalition, 1564 Lafond Ave., 646-1986.

Como

Boundaries: North: Hoyt Ave., Larpenteur Ave. **West:** Snelling Ave.
South: B.N. Railroad, Como Park, West Maryland Ave. **East:** Lexington
Parkway, Dale St.

To the northeast of the Midway is an expanse of woods and green space
with Lake Como as its centerpiece. Como Park is the jewel of northern
St. Paul, with a regal domed conservatory, zoo and older Victorian houses built along its borders. Its beginnings were more modest, however. In
1873, the city of St. Paul bought Lake Como and the land around it for
$100,000. A city halfway house was among the first buildings to go up on
the land; ex-inmates planted trees and tended flower beds as part of their
boarding obligation. A Japanese flower garden, band pavilion, and plant
conservatory were eventually added as more people began to visit Lake
Como for picnics and relaxation. In the 1860s, St. Paul's first mass transit
system, the horse drawn buses of the St. Paul Omnibus Lines, made
regular runs up to the lake in the summer. Como Park is just as popular
today. Besides a grandiose zoo and conservatory, the park has a public
swimming pool, golf course, and miles of paved trails.

Households are generally more affluent here than in surrounding
neighborhoods; median income is comparable to that of Mac-Groveland
and Highland to the south. A row of impressive 19th-century Victorian
homes overlooks the southern shore of Lake Como. Even so, many
homes were built in the 1940s, including moderately-priced bungalows
close to Snelling Avenue. A building boom in the 1970s also created
many additional houses in the neighborhood.

The perks of the Midway commercial district are not far away from the
Como neighborhood, but there's also a large shopping center closer to
home. Bandana Square, on Energy Park Drive just west of Lexington Parkway, contains several chain stores and specialty boutiques ideal for newcomers looking for interesting housewares and other moving-in needs.

Como adjoins the State Fairgrounds, and as a result it experiences a
wave of temporary visitors around the Labor Day weekend from the Minnesota State Fair. With its stock animal contests, thrill rides and concerts, the State Fair is highly recommended as a dose of Minnesota tradition. And, while the idea of living next to such an extravaganza may put
some people off, keep in mind that it only lasts a few weeks of the year.
Some enterprising Como residents even turn their location into dollars by
offering parking spaces on their front yard for a premium price.

Area Code: 612

Zip Codes: 55103, 55108, 55117

Post Offices: Como Station, 2286 Como Ave. Rice St. Station, 40 Arlington Ave. East. (All post office branches can be reached at 349-4711.)
Police: Western District Patrol Team, North: 292-3512, South: 292-3549.

Emergency Hospital: United Hospital, 333 Smith Ave. North, 220-8000.

Library: Hamline Branch, 1558 Minnehaha Ave. West, 292-6632.

Bus Lines: 5: State Fairgrounds/Downtown/Inver Grove Heights. **12:** Rosedale/Downtown/Stillwater. **17:** Dale St./Rosedale. **95E:** Downtown Minneapolis/Energy Park Dr./Downtown St. Paul.

Neighborhood Organization:
Como Community Council, 1556 Como Avenue, 644-3889.

West Seventh

Boundaries: North: I-35E. **West:** I-35E, Homer St. **South:** Mississippi River. **East:** West Kellogg Boulevard.

Just to the west of Downtown is St. Paul's old Uppertown, named for the upper of two boat landings that were alive with bustle and commerce in the mid-19th century. This neighborhood was where the first upscale St. Paulites spent their wealth by building tall, sturdy Victorian style homes with posted front porches, similar to those in old sections of many other towns along the Mississippi. As a result, there are more houses built before the Civil War in the West Seventh Street neighborhood than any-where else in St. Paul. Irvine Park, a National Historic District, includes Governor Alexander Ramsey's stone two-story house surrounded by an English garden. There are also some restored red brick rowhouses in this quiet enclave just west of Downtown.

As St. Paul expanded, West Seventh Street (then known as Fort Road for its access to Fort Snelling) became the destination of workers arriving from Europe. Beginning in the 1870s, Czech immigrants settled the neighborhood in search of jobs on railroads and in grain mills. As late as the 1950s, two to three hundred people gathered every month for screenings of Czech-language movies at the Garden Theater on Seventh Street. Poles, too, began moving to the neighborhood in the late 19th century, and Saint Stanislaus Catholic Church still stands on Superior Street as reminder of their presence. Another part of the history of West

Seventh has been washed away, literally. As early as the 1850s, Italian families built houses in the levee below Seventh Street right along the river (the site of today's Shepard Road). Their community, with its flocks of chickens and community ovens, was evacuated after it was inundated by a series of floods. Cossetta's Restaurant on West Seventh, whose owners moved it from a storefront location in the flood plain, has an awning reminding all that it is "Just a piece of the levee."

Today's West Seventh Street neighborhood certainly does not possess the excitement it did 100 years ago. The supper clubs, corner bars and second hand stores along West Seventh can have an almost ghostly feel. But this neighborhood should not be overlooked. The area offers a variety of starter home possibilities (particularly if you are not afraid of rehabbing) and housing prices are among the lowest in St. Paul. There are small, quiet blocks of modest Midwestern-square houses, mixed with brick worker's cottages and a few Victorian brick houses north of West Seventh with quick access to Grand Avenue shopping up the hill. South of West Seventh and west of Smith Avenue lies a stretch of simple, affordable, Victorians near the steep precipice of the Mississippi bluff. Those interested in restoration work may find this quarter quite attractive. If you visit the neighborhood and get hungry, you can get a bite to eat at the Day By Day Cafe.

Area Code: 612

Zip Codes: 55102, 55116

Post Offices: Main Office, 180 East Kellogg Boulevard.
Elway Station, 1715 West 7th St. (All post office branches can be reached at 349-4711.)

Police: Central District Patrol Team, 292-3563.

Emergency Hospital: United Hospital, 333 Smith Ave.
North, 220-8000.

Library: Central, 90 West 4th St., 292-6311.

Bus Lines: 3: Grand Ave./Downtown/3M Center. **9:** Highland Park/W. 7th St./Maplewood Mall. **10:** Highland Park/W. 7th St./Hillcrest Center. **14:** Ford Plant/W. 7th St./Hillcrest Center. Numerous routes run on I-35E, including the 54 Express to the International Airport and Mall of America.

Neighborhood Organization:
West Seventh Fort Road Federation, 974 West 7th Street, 298-5599.

Summit-University

Boundaries: North: University Ave. **West:** Lexington Parkway.
South: Summit Ave. **East:** Irvine Ave., Marion St.

If you're on Summit Avenue and head northward on Dale Street, you enter an area of once-upon grandeur and more recent urban neglect. Much like Summit Hill to its south, the Summit-University neighborhood contains many of the city's oldest buildings, including stone rowhouses, fortress-like Victorian woodframes, and elegant 19th-century brick store-fronts at the bottom of Selby Avenue. Unfortunately, Summit-University (or "Summit-U"), was decimated in the 1950s when planners routed Inter-state 94 directly down Rondo Avenue, through what was then a thriving, mixed-income African-American community. Many of Rondo's less well-off residents relocated southward, to form a concentration of lower-income housing in Summit-University.

Don't get the idea that Summit-U is a forgotten neighborhood, though. Numerous community initiatives and revitalization projects have taken place over the years. Summit-U is home to the Martin Luther King Center, which provides day care services and other activities. The well-known Penumbra Theater, which features plays with African-American themes, operates out of the MLK Center. The neighborhood is integrat-ed, with roughly equal parts white and African-American as well as a substantial Hmong-American population.

Many buildings have undergone restoration in Summit-U, particularly just north of Summit Avenue and along lower Selby. Although restora-tions along lower Selby have not developed into a full-scale neighbor-hood renaissance, the district offers several specialty shops, restaurants and pubs, with the grandeur of St. Paul's Cathedral nearby. Although incomes are generally lower in Summit-U than in other areas, profession-als and others with higher incomes have invested in houses here. If you're accustomed to the usual security precautions that are necessary in an urban area, you may want to consider Summit-U.

Area Code: 612

Zip Codes: 55102, 55103, 55104

Post Office: Industrial Station, 1430 Concordia Ave. (All post office branches can be reached at 349-4711.)

Police: Western District Patrol Team, North: 292-3512,
South: 292-3549.

Emergency Hospital: United Hospital, 333 Smith Ave.
North, 220-8000.

Library: Lexington Branch, 1080 University Ave. West, 292-6620.

Bus Lines: 3: Grand Ave./Downtown/3M Center. **16:** Downtown Minneapolis/University Ave./Downtown St. Paul. **17:** Dale St./Rosedale. **21:** Downtown/Selby Ave./Lake St. (Minneapolis). **22:** St. Anthony Ave./Downtown/St. Paul-Ramsey Medical Center.

Neighborhood Organization:
Summit-University Planning Council, 627 Selby Avenue, 228-1855.

Thomas-Dale (Frogtown)

Boundaries: North: B.N. Railroad. **West:** Lexington Parkway. **South:** University Ave. **East:** I-35E.

Along with Summit-University, the Thomas-Dale neighborhood forms the other half of St. Paul's urban core. Nobody knows for sure where its other name—Frogtown—comes from, although chances are it has to do with the neighborhood's earliest residents. No, not the French, the aquatic amphibians. In the 1880s, when Germans first settled this area northwest of the Capitol to be near rail yard jobs, they called their marshy new home, Froschburg, or Frog City, probably for their croaking companions outside, although the debate over the name rages on. Today, the marshes, with their frog choruses, are long gone.

The houses of Thomas-Dale are mostly quite modest consisting of worker cottages built by the earliest residents and newer two-story Midwestern squares. Some of the lots are rather narrow, apparently the result of subdivision by enterprising residents. Over half of the housing is pre-1940, and many of the cottages are over one hundred years old. Household incomes and house values here are the lowest in St. Paul, and, perhaps as a result, Thomas-Dale has always been a favorite neighborhood for newcomers of modest means, beginning with the European workers who settled Froschburg in the nineteenth century. More recently, African-American residents from the old Rondo neighborhood (see Summit-University) moved here. Most recently, refugees from the Vietnam War, including a quarter of the city's Hmong-American residents, have made Thomas-Dale their home.

The ethnic diversity in Thomas-Dale has brought a variety of businesses to the area. A Vietnamese business district, including scores of restaurants and bilingual services, runs along eastern University Avenue. The Blues Saloon on Western Avenue is a well-known club that attracts roots blues acts. A monument to the early European workers in the area is the Church of St. Agnes, with its 200-foot high onion dome roof. Overall, this area is recommended to newcomers only if they are used to the energy of an urban neighborhood.

Area Code: 612

Zip Codes: 55103, 55104

Post Offices: Rice St. Station, 40 Arlington Ave. East. Industrial Station, 1430 Concordia Ave. (All post office branches can be reached at 349-4711.)

Police: West of Rice St.: Western District Patrol Team, North: 292-3512, South: 292-3549. East of Rice St.: Central District Patrol Team, 292-3563.

Emergency Hospital: St. Paul-Ramsey Medical Center, 640 Jackson St., 221-3456.

Library: Lexington Branch, 1080 University Ave. West, 292-6620.

Bus Lines: 5: Inver Grove Heights/Como Blvd./State Fairgrounds. **7:** Thomas Ave./Downtown/Signal Hills. **8:** Jackson St./Inver Hills College. **12:** Downtown/ Rice St./Stillwater. **16:** Downtown Minneapolis/University Ave./Downtown St. Paul. **17:** Dale St./Rosedale. **95E:** Downtown/Como Blvd./U. of M. Lexington Line: Lexington/Little Canada. Hodgson Line: Rice St./Circle Pines. Rice Street Line: Rice St./Cty. Rd. B.

Neighborhood Organization:
Thomas-Dale Planning Council, 369 University Ave., 298-5068.

North End

Boundaries: North: Larpenteur Ave. **West:** Dale St., Lexington Parkway. **South:** B.N. Railroad. **East:** I-35E.

Heading north from the State Capitol on Rice Street, you cross the railroad tracks and enter the city's North End, which includes an old working-class enclave with some elegant pillared Victorian woodframes in the southern half, and a region with a suburban feel to the north. Many of the small hundred-year-old houses to the south were built by rail yard and mill workers during St. Paul's population boom at the end of the 19th century.

The North End is modest but not monotonous, with tidy homes and considerable variety in ethnicity, age and income. A sizable number of residents are over 65, and fifteen percent are Asian-American. The neighborhood's older, blue-collar section centers around two large cemeteries, Oakland (the city's oldest) and Calvary. Besides the Victorian houses, many sturdy Midwestern square-style houses and small worker cottages line the streets. The northern stretch of residences surrounding Wheelock Parkway, extending to the east toward Lake Phalen, make up the neighborhood's more affluent section. Large, pre-1940 Midwestern square and Colonial style houses are interspersed with more recently-built split-levels. Wheelock Parkway winds through the North End, following the edge of a sheer bluff overlooking another cemetery (Elmhurst) and the plain below.

The three neighborhoods that make up St. Paul's northeastern corner—North End, Payne-Phalen and Hayden Heights—are similar in many ways. They are all stable, pleasant places to live, populated by families and older residents, with moderate house values and household incomes. In fact, the tracts here of recently-built houses and rolling hills have more in common with the surrounding suburb of Maplewood than with St. Paul. Convenience shopping is available on thoroughfares such as Rice Street, and Maplewood Mall is a short drive north of the city on White Bear Avenue. The only negative is that residents are somewhat cut off from the life of the city (although, depending on what you're looking for, you may see this isolation as an asset). If you're thinking suburban but want (or need) a relatively quick drive into downtown St. Paul, consider the northeastern neighborhoods.

Area Code: 612

Zip Codes: 55101, 55103, 55117

Post Office: Rice St. Station, 40 Arlington Ave. East. (All post office branches can be reached at 349-4711.)

Police: West of Rice St.: Western District Patrol Team, North: 292-3512, South: 292-3549. East of Rice St.: Central District Patrol Team, 292-3563.

Emergency Hospital: St. Paul-Ramsey Medical Center, 640 Jackson St., 221-3456.

Library: Rice St. Branch, 995 Rice St., 292-6630.

Bus Lines: 5: Inver Grove Heights/Como Blvd./State Fairgrounds. **8:** Jackson St./Inver Hills College. **12:** Downtown/Rice St./Stillwater. **17:** Dale St./Rosedale. **95E:** Downtown/Como Blvd./U. of M. Lexington Line: Lexington/Little Canada. Hodgson Line: Rice St./Circle Pines. Rice Street Line: Rice St./Cty. Rd. B.

Neighborhood Organization:
District 6 Planning Council, 1053 North Dale Street, 488-4485.

Payne-Phalen

Boundaries: North: Larpenteur Ave. **West:** I-35E. **South:** Grove St., B.N Railroad. **East:** Johnson Parkway, McAfee St.

The Payne-Phalen neighborhood epitomizes the modesty of St. Paul in comparison to its glitzier neighbor to the west. Houses along the shores of Lake Phalen, consisting of two-story woodframes and simple bungalows, with few Honeywell security signs, iron fences, or lights illuminating the underbrush, are simpler and smaller than the opulent spreads that surround Minneapolis lakes. Even houses along Wheelock Parkway, an elegant boulevard, are distinctly low-key. The neighborhood has a quiet charm, however. Lake Phalen is spacious, surrounded by a substantial expanse of rolling hills, a golf course, elm-shaded bluffs and a paved running path. In the summer you can rent sailboats here and in the winter, the park offers cross country ski lessons.

Residential areas around Lake Phalen are in many ways similar to the North End: pleasantly modest homes, with substantial numbers of older residents. Payne-Phalen is over 80 percent white, with more African-American, Asian-American, Native-American, and Hispanic-American residents living in the working-class section centered around Payne Avenue to the south. Bungalows and Midwestern square-style houses (as well as a scattering of unique turn-of-the-century Victorian houses) are to be found on the southern end, and rows of larger Colonial houses and bungalows line the gradual slope toward Lake Phalen. Stability is the key selling point here. Church groups, bowling leagues, and youth hockey games are popular activities. If you're looking for a quiet place to live where neighbors look out for each other, consider Payne-Phalen.

Area Code: 612

Zip Codes: 55101, 55106

Post Offices: Dayton Bluff Station, 1425 Minnehaha Ave. East. Seeger Square Station, 886 Arcade St. (All post office branches can be reached at 349-4711.)

Police: Eastern District Patrol Team, 292-3565.

Emergency Hospital: St. Paul-Ramsey Medical Center, 640 Jackson St., 221-3456.

Library: Arlington Hills, 1105 Greenbrier St., 292-6637.

Bus Lines: 8: Westminster St./Downtown/Inver Hills.
10: Highland Park/Arcade St./Hillcrest Center. **11:** Maplewood Mall/Payne Ave./Inver Hills. **14:** Hillcrest/Payne Ave./Ford Plant.
15: Downtown/Arcade St./Mahtomedi. A Park N' Ride lot is at Larpenteur Ave. and Arcade St.

Neighborhood Organization:
District 5 Planning Council, 1014 Payne Ave., 774-5234.

Dayton's Bluff

Boundaries: North: Grove St., B. N. Railroad. **West:** Lafayette Rd, State Highway 3. **South:** Warner Rd. **East:** U.S. Highway 61, Birmingham St., Hazelwood St., Johnson Parkway.

At East Seventh Street and Minnehaha Avenue, atop a bluff to the east of Downtown, one of St. Paul's earliest upscale neighborhoods rises above the city. In the 1850s, land speculator Lyman Dayton built a house on this land and named the spot Dayton's Bluff (what else?). Today many Victorian-style homes still stand here, somewhat forlornly, waiting for restoration. In addition, there are numerous smaller square wood-frames, built by workers who moved here in the 1880s.

The neighborhood is now solidly blue-collar, with modest house values and incomes, plenty of families, and workers engaged in assembly, repair or technical jobs at one of the industrial areas nearby. Neighborhood taverns light up many corners, mixed with strip malls, convenience stores and department stores along Minnehaha Avenue. Although a few of the stately Victorian houses have received a new paint job and restoration, Dayton's Bluff remains for the most part a renaissance-in-waiting. Streets that were once traveled by elegant carriages are now dotted with occasional boarded-up or neglected houses.

At the southern end of Dayton's Bluff is a steep hilltop with a breathtaking view of the Mississippi River Valley and both downtowns. As early as 1,000 B.C., the Hopewell Indians chose it as a burial site, leaving behind a series of oval-shaped burial mounds along the edge of the bluff. The overlook, with the six grave sites that remain, is now Indian Mounds Park, complete with walkways around the mounds, picnic areas and playgrounds.

Area Code: 612

Zip Codes: 55101, 55106

Post Offices: Dayton's Bluff Station, 1425 Minnehaha Ave. East. Main Office, 180 E. Kellogg Blvd. (All post office branches can be reached at 349-4711.)
Police: Eastern District Patrol Team, 292-3565.

Emergency Hospital: St. Paul-Ramsey Medical Center, 640 Jackson St., 221-3456.

Libraries: Arlington Hills, 1105 Greenbrier St., 292-6637. Sun Ray Branch, 2105 Wilson Ave., 292-6640.

Bus Lines: 3: Grand Ave./E. 3rd St./3M Center. **9:** Highland Park/ E. 7th St./Maplewood. **12:** Rosedale/E. 6th St./Stillwater.

49: Downtown/Burns Ave./Sun Ray Center. **61:** Downtown/U.S. Hwy. 61/Cottage Grove.

Neighborhood Organization:
Dayton's Bluff Center for Civic Life, 281 Maria Ave., 772-2075.

West Side

Boundaries: North-West-East: Mississippi River. **South:** Annapolis St.

Cross the arching Smith Avenue High Bridge, and you're in St. Paul's West Side. The neighborhood actually lies directly south of Downtown; its name apparently has something to do with being tucked into the opposite side of a bend in the Mississippi, a river which, for the most part, separates east from west. But there's nothing disorienting about the West Side—few neighborhoods in the Twin Cities are more stable or diverse or as good a place for families. On a summer evening, a park may have the sounds of a Little League game, an adult softball tournament, or a Central-American League intramural soccer match.

The bluff area was once a sprawling farm, so the earliest buildings on the West Side are farmhouses and workers' cottages from the mid-19th century. Many of the other houses are Midwestern squares and variations on bungalows, occasionally intermingled with newer split levels. Home values and incomes on the West Side are slightly below midrange in St. Paul, comparable to those in the North End and Payne-Phalen. The neighborhood is neither solidly working-class nor exclusively professional; residents are employed in a mix of service and manufacturing occupations. The blocks west of Smith Avenue directly across from Cherokee Park are more stately, with larger Colonials, Tudors and bungalows. These quiet streets are only a short walk to the park's spacious bluffside views. Set atop a steep sandstone bluff, Cherokee Park offers an awesome panorama of river barges and downtown St. Paul.

Across the neighborhood, centering around Concord Street, is the Twin Cities' largest Hispanic-American district. The Mexicans, Puerto Ricans, Cubans and Central Americans of the area make up more than twenty percent of the West Side's population. Mexicans first came to the area in the early 1900s for migrant jobs at northern sugar beet farms, and later, for industrial jobs in nearby South St. Paul and elsewhere. More recently, Central Americans fleeing war and poverty have moved to this neighborhood. You can find numerous places to get enchiladas and margaritas along Concord and Robert Streets, or visit an excellent supermercado and deli, El Burrito, which has enough bright colors and zesty food delights to overcome any case of the winter blues. In May, Concord Street's Cinco de Mayo festival draws thousands of revelers, musicians and crafts vendors.

Heading southward, Robert Street becomes a commercial district, with warehouse food outlets, department stores and restaurants. Everything from housewares to used cars can be found on South Robert Street. On the far eastern side of the neighborhood, on the flats across the river from Downtown, is Holman Field, a small airplane landing strip used mostly by charter and private flyers.

The bluffs of Cherokee Park offer a great place for solitude, and an occasional glimpse of the river's wildlife. Bird watchers can spot herons and egrets riding updrafts over the bluff's edge and, once in a great while, a bald eagle perched on a branch or soaring overhead. Below the bluffs are the sandstone walls and marshy river flats of Lilydale Park, which contain small caves and indentations in the bluffs created by eons of percolation and erosion. At the turn of the century, some of the caves were used by Yoerg's Brewery for cold storage of their beer barrels which were subsequently marketed as "Yoerg's Cave-Aged Picnic Beer." Nearly all of the cave openings are now barred up because of cave-ins and other accidents, but the foundations of the brewery, the ruins of an old brick foundry, and the massive cottonwoods standing along the Mississippi flats still make for interesting exploring.

Area Code: 612

Zip Code: 55107

Post Office: Riverview Station, 292 Eva St. (All post office branches can be reached at 349-4711.)

Police: Central District Patrol Team, 292-3565.

Emergency Hospitals: St. Paul-Ramsey Medical Center, 640 Jackson St., 221-3456. HealthEast St. Joseph's Hospital, 69 West Exchange St., 232-3000.

Library: Riverview Branch, 1 East George St., 292-6626.

Bus Lines: 5: State Fairgrounds/Stryker Ave./Inver Grove Heights. 7: Downtown/Smith Ave./S. Robert St. 8: Downtown/S. Robert St./Inver Hills. 11: Little Canada/Concord St./Inver Hills. 29: Downtown/Riverview Industrial Park. 95U, M: West St. Paul Target Park N' Ride/U. of M./Downtown Minneapolis.

Neighborhood Organization:
West Side Citizens' Organization, 625 Stryker Ave., 293-1708.

Hayden Heights, Hazel Park, Prosperity Park, Hillcrest

Boundaries: North: Larpenteur Ave. **West**: Hazelwood St., Johnson Parkway, McAfee St. **South**: East Minnehaha Ave. **East: McKnight Rd.**

Driving up the gradual slope of Minnehaha Avenue and crossing White Bear Avenue, one comes upon a plateau of mid- to small post-1940s bungalows and ramblers on quiet streets shaded by relatively young trees. This is Hayden Heights, which, together with several other small subdivisions, composes the northeastern corner of the city. It is a tranquil residential area with a mix of young families and retirees.

The difference in appearance between this northeastern corner of St. Paul with its post-World War II suburban style houses and the older adjacent neighborhoods is dramatic. Incomes and house values are only slightly higher here than in Payne-Phalen and Dayton's Bluff but the small, well-tended yards and quiet enclaves have more in common with the more upscale suburb of Maplewood next door than with most of St. Paul. There is a sprinkling of African-American, Hmong and Laotian residents in this largely white community.

Surrounding the area to the north and east is Maplewood, the relatively affluent suburban home to 3M Company's international headquarters. Hayden Heights residents can enjoy some of the commercial amenities of living next to a well-off suburb, including Maplewood Mall, a large indoor shopping center to the north, and Maplewood Bowl, an entertainment center that hosts live music shows. Hayden Heights has several small parks, and Lake Phalen is close enough to the neighborhood for easy visits.

Area Code: 612

Zip Codes: 55106, 55119

Post Office: Eastern Heights Station, 1910 Suburban Ave. (All post office branches can be reached at 349-4711.)

Police: Eastern District Patrol Team, 292-3565.

Emergency Hospital: St. Paul-Ramsey Medical Center, 640 Jackson St., 221-3456.

Library: Hayden Heights Branch, 1456 White Bear Ave. N., 292-6646.

Bus Lines: 9: Downtown/White Bear Ave./Oakdale. **10:** Highland Park/Maryland Ave./Hillcrest Center. **12:** Rosedale/Minnehaha Ave./Stillwater. **14:** Highland Park/Maryland Ave./Hillcrest Center. **20:** Maplewood Mall/White Bear Ave./Sun Ray Center.

Neighborhood Organization:
District 2 Community Council, 2169 Stillwater Ave., 731-6842.

Sunray, Battlecreek, Highwood

Boundaries: North: Minnehaha Ave. **West:** Hazelwood St., Birmingham St., Warner Rd. **South:** Mississippi River, city limits. **East:** McKnight Rd.

Sunray-Battlecreek-Highwood the wide expanse that makes up St. Paul's southeastern corner, does not contain as much housing as one might think. Much of this area instead consists of the wetlands of Pig's Eye Lake Park and Battle Creek Park, as well as a railroad and industrial zone that occupies a slice of land along State Highway 61. The houses that are here have been built mostly since the 1950s, especially during a building boom in the 1970s, and as a result the neighborhood has the newer look of nearby Maplewood and Woodbury. The exception to this suburban appearance is the northwestern corner of Sunray, which is made up of simple, turn-of-the century bungalows and Midwestern-square wood frame houses, much like adjacent Dayton's Bluff.

Many Sunray residents are professionals, others work in service and retail jobs. The neighborhood is youthful—many residents have young children—and primarily white with approximately ten percent African-American and Mexican-American residents. Prices for the tidy houses, condos, and townhouses of Sunray are above average for St. Paul, comparable to house values in Merriam Park and Como but well below the most expensive Twin Cities neighborhoods. Houses also tend to be less expensive than in the nearby suburban communities of Maplewood and Woodbury, so living here can save you money while offering the same lifestyle as in those suburbs.

Despite its isolated location, Sunray-Battlecreek-Highwood is close to shopping possibilities along Interstate 94, among them the Sun Ray Shopping Center and the Horizon Outlet Center, a mall containing more than fifty factory outlet stores. Ample hiking and biking areas can be found along the rocky bed of Battle Creek Park and at other green spaces in the neighborhood. Across State Highway 61 from Battle Creek, Pig's Eye Lake Park is home to nesting great blue herons, egrets and cormorants. Access to Pig's Eye Lake (actually a backwater of the Mississippi) is limited to one dead-end road some distance from most of the nesting grounds, but a pair of binoculars can bring you closer to the birds on the remote shores of Pig's Eye.

Area Code: 612

Zip Codes: 55106, 55119

Post Office: Eastern Heights Station, 1910 Suburban Ave. (All post office branches can be reached at 349-4711.)

Police: Eastern District Patrol Team, 292-3565.

Emergency Hospital: St. Paul-Ramsey Medical Center, 640 Jackson St., 221-3456.

Library: Sun Ray Branch, 2105 Wilson Ave., 292-6640.

Bus Lines: 3: Grand Ave./Sun Ray Center/3M Center. **12:** Rosedale/Minnehaha Ave./Stillwater. **20:** Maplewood Mall/White Bear Ave./Sun Ray Center. **49:** Downtown/Sun Ray Center/3M Center. **61:** Downtown/U.S. Hwy. 61/Cottage Grove. Numerous **94** routes run along I-94 to eastern suburbs.

Neighborhood Organization:
District 1 Community Council, 2090 Conway St., Rm. 126, 292-7828.

Surrounding Communities

Today, the Twin Cities are much more than just the metropolitan boundaries of Minneapolis and St. Paul. The post World War II baby boom followed by the rapid expansion in the 1960s of the Interstate highway system, led to enormous migration of new families into what had been farms and forests. In fact, over the past fifty years or so the metro area has grown into an amorphous expanse that includes more than eighty distinct suburban communities, some of them now serving as mini-centers for even more distant suburbs.

The 1990 census revealed that virtually all of the Twin Cities' growth has been in the suburbs, and two-thirds of Minnesota's population growth since 1990 has taken place in eight suburban Twin Cities counties. The appetite for new land is voracious and not letting up: latest expansion is to the east in Washington County, and even across the Wisconsin state line in Pierce and St. Croix Counties, which are now considered part of the metro area. There's also been rapid growth in outlying communities to the northwest, such as Coon Rapids, and southwest, such as Eden Prairie. More established inner-ring communities such as Bloomington, St. Louis Park and Golden Valley remain vital and show no sign of losing people either.

The attraction of the surrounding communities is obvious: quiet, wooded streets, new buildings, an occasional deer in the backyard. Breaking new ground out on the edges has always been irresistible for Americans in search of their own space. There are both brand-new suburbs and long established ones: Apple Valley was little more than farm fields thirty years ago whereas Anoka, an old river city, has a historic downtown and many elegant Victorian houses. Furthermore, the monotony of the post World War II bedroom communities has in many places given way to vibrant suburbs that offer a variety of services, reasonable dining options, and even Starbuck's Coffee shops. One important consideration to keep in mind as you choose where to live: if you don't own an automobile, mass transit is sparse to non-existent in many outlying communities, although some of the suburbs are served by metro bus lines and Park N' Ride lots that can connect you to city buses. Check this book's **Transportation** section for further information.

Below are phone numbers to call for information on outlying communities. Generally, the numbers given are for city offices, although a few are for Chambers of Commerce.

Southern Suburbs
Apple Valley. 932-2500
Bloomington. 948-8700
Burnsville. 895-4400
Eagan 681-4600
Inver Grove Heights. 450-2500
Lakeville. 469-4431
Mendota Heights 452-1850
Prior Lake 447-4230
Richfield. 861-9700
Rosemount 423-4411
Savage. 882-2660
Shakopee. 445-3650
South St. Paul 450-8733
West St. Paul. 552-4100

Western Suburbs
Chanhassen. 937-1900
Chaska. 448-2851
Crystal 531-1000
Dayton 427-4589
Eden Prairie. 949-8300
Edina 927-8861
Golden Valley 593-8000
Hopkins 935-8474
Maple Grove 420-4000
Minnetonka 939-8200
New Hope 531-5110
Plymouth 509-5000
Robbinsdale. 537-4534
St. Louis Park 924-2500
Wayzata. 473-0234

Northern Suburbs
Andover 755-5100
Anoka. 421-6630
Arden Hills 633-5676
Blaine. 784-6700
Brooklyn Center. 569-3300
Brooklyn Park 493-8000

Champlin 421-8100
Circle Pines 784-5898
Columbia Heights 782-2800
Coon Rapids 755-2880
Falcon Heights. 644-5050
Fridley 571-3450
Ham Lake 434-9555
Lino Lakes 464-5562
Little Canada 484-2177
Mounds View. 784-3055
New Brighton. 638-2100
Roseville 490-2200
Shoreview 490-4600
Spring Lake Park. 784-6491
St. Anthony 789-8881
Vadnais Heights. 429-5343

Eastern Suburbs
Cottage Grove 458-2800
Hastings. 437-4127
Lake Elmo 777-5510
Mahtomedi. 426-3344
Maplewood 770-4500
North St. Paul 770-4450
Oakdale. 739-5086
Stillwater 439-6121
White Bear Lake 429-8526
Woodbury 739-5972

Twin Cities Address Locator

There are places where Twin Cities streets follow a perfect grid, and places where streets are laid out at crazy angles with no sense to east, west, north or south. The convolutions are primarily due to the Mississippi winding through both downtowns with no concern for the needs of city planners. City boundaries—where streets may change names abruptly—add additional confusion. Suburban communities often follow Twin Cities street patterns, but not always. For the full picture, you'll need to accompany this guide with a map. Even better is a hefty street atlas, which offers page-by-page micro-views of every metropolitan block accompanied by an index of all streets. With one in hand, keep the following things in mind:

Minneapolis

- Street addresses are uniformly divided in hundreds, block by block. Numbers increase moving outward from the Mississippi River on the north side and from Nicollet Avenue on the south side.

- Downtown streets are laid out diagonally to the compass (the pesky Mississippi!), so try not to let compass directions throw you off. Because of their orientation to the river, numbered streets and those running parallel to them are labeled north or south, dividing at Hennepin Avenue.

- South Minneapolis (south of Grant Street) is straightforward and easy to understand. Numbered streets run east-west, with ascending numbers going southward. Avenues for the most part run north-south, and have numbers east of Nicollet Avenue and proper names west of Nicollet. So, in South Minneapolis, the higher the numbered street, the further south it is; the higher the numbered avenue, the further east it is.

- In the University of Minnesota neighborhood, numbered streets generally run east-west, while numbered avenues run north-south. Streets and avenues here are labeled Southeast.

- Northeast Minneapolis: numbered avenues run east-west, with numbers ascending northward. North-south streets are numbered heading east of the river until 6th Street. East of 6th the streets are named chronologically after U.S. presidents, from Washington to Coolidge.

- North Minneapolis: numbered avenues run east-west, with numbers ascending northward. North-south streets have ascending numbers as you go west of the Mississippi, until 7th Street. West of 7th, streets have proper names.

St. Paul

- Along with St. Paul's Old-World charm comes a somewhat confusing street system. St. Paul's street numbers don't always follow tidy increments of one hundred for every block; they may change from 100 to 200 in the middle of the block so . . . get out that atlas.

- West of Downtown, the north-south dividing line is Summit Avenue. Street numbers increase going westward from Downtown.
- Downtown, Wabasha Street is the division between east and west. The Mississippi River is the north-south marker.

- East of Downtown the north-south dividing line is Upper Afton Road. Street numbers increase going eastward from Downtown.

- Some roads have numbered names Downtown and on the east side, but since they're not numbered in relation to anything else, the numbers don't assist much in orientation.

From City to City

- University and Franklin Avenues keep their names going from St. Paul to Minneapolis, but Marshall Avenue in St. Paul becomes Lake Street in Minneapolis, and St. Paul's Ford Parkway becomes 46th Street in Minneapolis. Don't worry too much, there are only a handful of these streets to remember. The river breaks most of them up.

- Some suburbs, especially inner ones, number their streets according to the grid of the Twin Cities. Other older or far-flung suburbs, such as Wayzata, are laid out on their own grid. The simple advice: don't expect address numbers in the 'burbs and cities to match up.

All in all, the Twin Cities are no more difficult to navigate than any other middle-aged American city with a few geographical quirks. Take a few trips to different parts of town and it won't be long before you're tooling around like a native.

You should have little trouble finding a place to rent in the Twin Cities—there's no shortage of rental property, and rents are still reasonable (though on the rise, as noted in a recent survey which showed that apartment rents in the Twin Cities increased an average of 5.1% from one year to the next, nearly twice the rate of inflation). Even apartments in the most popular neighborhoods are not outrageously expensive, although vacancies may be more scarce. With a little persistence, however, you should be able find a handsome turn-of-the-century brick and stone apartment in Uptown or near Grand Avenue, two of the most popular neighborhoods for newcomers.

If you are looking to buy rather than rent, rest assured that in the Twin Cities you'll be getting value for your dollar: according to a 1995 National Association of Home Builders study, Minneapolis-St. Paul was ranked as one of the 25 most affordable housing markets in the country. Another recent study reported that the average share of household income required for monthly house payments in the Twin Cities was a relatively low 17%. Of course, it won't last: to wit, the real-estate board for Minneapolis-St. Paul reported that in 1996 the average sale price for a house in the Twin Cities was $130,000, up 11% over the previous year, far outstripping the inflation rate. Still, the Twin Cities offer prospective homeowners great housing buys, particularly when one takes into account the high quality of life here.

In many ways, the Twin Cities are a "big small town" which means you can easily find an apartment on your own. Of course, if that's not for you, you can let a professional find you a place to live. Should you decide to do your own footwork, check this guide's neighborhood descriptions to learn about the types of housing in different parts of town. The neighborhood organizations listed in the profiles are excellent resources to call if you've got your eye on an apartment. They can give you a level-headed assessment of the neighborhood. You can also call the police precinct that patrols the neighborhood you are interested in (the numbers are listed at the end of each neighborhood profile).

Most important, visit the neighborhood, perhaps have breakfast at a local restaurant, and tour around. Find out if services and conveniences you are used to having available are nearby. Pay attention to your comfort level. Some people are put off by noise or lots of people moving through the neighborhood; conversely some people are bothered if their home is isolated from the rest of civilization. All of these will be factors in your decision about where to live.

Here are some methods you may want to use in your hunt:

Classified Advertisements

Star Tribune - The Sunday *Star-Tribune* has the most comprehensive metro-area listings. Get it Saturday night at a convenience store to plan out a Sunday hunt.

St. Paul Pioneer Press - The better resource for St. Paul and the eastern metro area. The Sunday edition has the most listings.

City Pages, Twin Cities Reader - Free alternative weeklies, available at businesses metro-wide. Not extensive listings, but worth checking.

Neighborhood newspapers - Usually free at businesses and newsstands in the neighborhood. See *Skyway News* for listings in and near the downtowns. Also, many suburbs have their own newspapers for sale at area convenience stores.

Other Media

Look everywhere—on bulletin boards at cafes, laundermats, and on college campuses in the area you've got in mind. Answer "Roommate Wanted" ads if you don't mind sharing and you're on a tight budget. If you're connected to a college, check its housing referral service. Walk or drive around, watching carefully—some apartments are only advertised by a sign in the window. Here are some other options:

Free Rental Guides. A few companies publish free guides to large apartment complexes, condos and townhouses, available at metro businesses, bus stops and newspaper stands. The best-known is *Living Guide of the Twin Cities*, which has a useful cross-reference index of amenities and features for the rentals they list. They'll mail it to you free of charge. Call **858-8960**.

Star Tribune Fonahome - The "Strib" offers a free housing rental information service, including photos, floor plans, maps, and videos of some properties. Tell them your needs, and they'll send information by fax or overnight mail. Call **975-6168**, or **800-362-4663**.

The Internet - If you want to get an idea of the market before getting to the Twin Cities, you may want to subscribe to one of the city newspapers on-line for a month and check out their classifieds. There's more information on subscription rates and setup at the Worldwide Web sites of the two metro area dailies, listed below. If you're in the market to buy a home before you relocate here, hook into the third web site listed below. From it you can link to listings of homes, look up realtors, and even download photos of homes. Also, look up realtors' individual web sites through keywords such as "realty," "Minneapolis," and so on.

- **Star Tribune**, www.startribune.com
- **Pioneer Press**, www.pioneerplanet.com
- **Virtual Realty**, www.mnrealty.com

Apartment Search Firms

Many landlords lease their apartments through rental agents or apartment search firms. A search firm can be convenient if you have a limited amount of time to find a place to live. Agents are willing to fax you information, refer you to rental properties, or arrange appointments to show you places. When talking to a rental agent, be specific about your needs. This way you will not waste time considering places that aren't right for you. The following are some of the largest and most well-known apartment search firms. Their fee is typically paid by the property owners, so the service to you is free.

- **Apartment Mart**, Minneapolis: 927-4591, St. Paul: 224-9199
- **Apartment Referral, Inc.**, 800-899-5665
- **Apartment Search**, 800-989-4005

Temporary Housing

If you are in no hurry to find a long-term place to live, you may want to take a short-term sublet. Many such sublets are available in May, when students begin to leave town with time remaining on their leases. Apartment search firms can also be put to work to find a short-term place to stay. Of course, as a last resort, there's always your friend's couch. Check this book's Lodgings section for some affordable temporary options.

Considerations

Your housing search will be easier if you keep a few things in mind. First, ask yourself how much space you need. If you're alone, depending on your budget, you might consider a studio or efficiency instead of a one-bedroom apartment. Conversely, if you're looking with a partner, consider renting a two-bedroom—in the Twin Cities, they are often not much more expensive than one-bedrooms.

In Minnesota, an important question to ask is who will be paying for heat. If it's you and not the landlord, you'll be adding another 50 to 150 dollars a month to your cost of living during the cold months, depending on the size and insulation of the apartment. Landlord-paid heat does exist, though, particularly in apartment buildings. If you are curious, you can find out the average cost of utilities for a building by calling the utility that provides the gas service (most likely Northern States Power or Minnegasco—see the "Getting Settled" section).

Another consideration is the availability of parking. Off-street parking is especially desirable in the winter because you can ignore the city snowplow. Garage space is ideal—your car will stay warmer, and you won't have to scrape off ice and snow in the morning.

Take the opportunity to meet the landlord or agent to evaluate how he or she would be to rent from. Pay attention to the relationship between him or her and any current tenants (if you get the chance, privately ask the current tenants what it's like to rent from their landlord). A few other suggestions:

- Visit the actual unit you'll be renting, not "one just like it" in the same complex.

- Make sure that the landlord or building manager has a phone number and is available at any time. It's also a good idea to find out if a prospective landlord/manager has a history of complaints against them through a tenants' group (see below for listings).

- Check with the city's housing inspection department for past code violations.

- Watch for discrimination. In Minnesota, it's illegal to deny housing based on race, religion, or any other personal basis. Minneapolis specifically prohibits discrimination based on sexual orientation.

Security Deposits, Leases and Agreements

As a general rule, make sure you understand everything on the lease before you sign. Remember that a lease is a mutual agreement, and you can negotiate. Following are some clauses you should challenge or avoid:

- Unannounced entry. Minnesota recently enacted a law forbidding a landlord to enter an apartment without permission or reasonable notice (24 hours) except in emergencies.

- Responsibility for repairs without compensation. If you agree to perform any maintenance on your apartment, you can negotiate a rent decrease. Make sure it's in writing.
- Escalation and acceleration clauses. Some leases permit an owner

to raise the rent during a lease period (escalation). Other lease language may state that upon missing a month's rent, you are immediately liable for the rest of the lease amount, which could be thousands of dollars (acceleration). These kinds of clauses are legal, but you may not want to rent from some one proposing them. Pay attention and read the fine print.

Tenants' Rights

The above suggestions are a few broad guidelines, but you may want more detailed information. An excellent resource for learning your rights and responsibilities as a renter is a book called *The Tenants Rights Handbook*, a joint effort by three Minnesota consumer groups. It's available for only $5 from any of the tenants' unions listed below. These are also the organizations to turn to if have a problem with your landlord. The government offices listed below can also help out.

State of Minnesota Attorney General   296-3353
(offers advice, information)

City of Minneapolis Housing Services
8 a.m. to 4:30 p.m. weekdays   673-3003
First Call for Help (24 hours)   335-5000
(offers advice, refers city inspectors)

City of St. Paul Housing Information Office
8 a.m. to 4:30 p.m. weekdays   266-6000
First Call for Help (24 hours)   224-1133
(offers advice, refers city inspectors)

St. Paul Tenants Union   221-0501
500 Laurel Ave., St. Paul
(offers services for yearly membership fee: $7 to 18, sliding scale)

Minnesota Tenants Union
1513 Franklin Ave. E., Minneapolis   871-7485
Pay-per-call hotline (call office for details)   976-8888

Renter's Insurance

Get it. Most building owner's insurance does not cover your possessions or liability. Besides, renter's insurance is usually inexpensive and you can probably obtain it from the insurance agent who sold you your auto insurance. If you have a question regarding the integrity of a particular agent, call the Minnesota Department of Commerce, Division of Enforcement (296-2488) and they may be able to help.

Before buying renter's insurance, take an inventory of your possessions by making a list, taking photos, or videotaping all of your valuables, including furniture, electronics, jewelry and anything else of value. This will give you an idea of how much insurance you need as well as valuable documentation should you need to prove losses. Be sure to store this documentation in a secure place outside of your home, perhaps in a bank safe deposit box or with a friend.

One of the first things you'll do, even as you look for a place to live, is open a bank account. Some landlords and rental agents don't like to rent to people without a checking account, so it pays not to burn your financial bridges before leaving your old city. If you keep your old bank account for at least a short time after moving, it may help ease the transition to your new home.

When choosing a bank, some considerations in your decision might be physical convenience, banking hours, services required, interest rates offered and cost/fees. The largest Twin Cities banks have branches throughout the metro area, which can make them most convenient. You may, however, opt for a smaller community bank, of which there are plenty. Also, your place of work or your alma mater may offer membership in a credit union, which could be the best deal of all. To find out if you may be eligible for membership in a credit union, contact the National Association of Credit Unions at 608-231-4000.

Checking Accounts

Call around to ask about special promotions for opening new checking accounts—all of the largest banks regularly offer such perks as a free box of checks. A popular option most banks now have is the debit card. You can use it to withdraw money from your checking account at an automated teller machine (ATM), or you can make purchases with it directly, as with a credit card. Some banks also connect the debit card to a line of credit as overdraft protection. Cards are quickly becoming the way to bank, with banks encouraging people to use the cards instead of tellers for simple deposits and withdrawals. That aside, if you're coming from a large urban area, you'll probably be pleasantly surprised at how readily most Twin Cities merchants still accept personal checks.

To open an account, most banks require that you stop in with a minimum deposit (depending on the type of account you want, some have minimums as low as $50) and current photo identification. Below are five of the largest Twin Cities banks, each with scores of branches throughout the Twin Cities.

- **First Bank**, 244-3900
- **Firstar Bank (First Star Express Line)**, 784-5600
- **Marquette Bank**, 661-4000
- **Norwest**, 667-9378
- **Twin Cities Federal (TCF)**, 823-2265

Other Services

You may also want to open a savings account at the same time you do the checking account. Most banks will take care of both at the same time. Another thing to keep in mind: with the lines between banks, insurance companies and brokerage houses blurring, many banks are now active in a variety of financial arenas, and they may be able to offer you not just certificates of deposit but attractive money market accounts and even stock mutual funds. If these are relevant issues to you, it may be worth asking about them when deciding where to open your account.

Consumer Protection

If you have a problem with your bank, first try to resolve the matter by bringing it to the attention of a senior bank officer. It's in their interest to resolve the matter to the customer's satisfaction. If the problem is still not taken care of to your satisfaction, there are state and federal agencies that handle consumer complaints against banks. The first resource to use (for advice and referral elsewhere) is this state office: Minnesota Department of Commerce, Office of Enforcement, 133 E. 7th St., St. Paul, 296-2488.

Credit Cards

You won't have to live here long to begin accumulating a haystack of credit card applications with dynamic offers promising to outdo all others. If you want to get a credit card sooner, you can apply directly by using the following methods:

- **Visa** and **MasterCard:** hopefully, you're reading this before you've set up a bank account, because your bank probably offers both. You may choose the convenience of having this end of your finances under the same roof as others, but you can probably to find a better rate by shopping around.
- **American Express**, 800-THE-CARD
- **Diner's Club**, 800-2DINERS
- **Discover**, 800-347-2683 (or apply at Sears stores)
- **Department store credit card** applications can be obtained at the checkout counter, and stores frequently offer immediate discounts if

you apply for a card at the checkout. The most well-known local department store is Dayton's, with several locations metro-wide. Department store cards are easy to qualify for and can be used to establish a credit history if you have none.

Income Taxes

As a resident here, you will have to pay federal and state income taxes.

- **Federal Tax Forms**, 800-829-FORM (or stop by a public library or post office)
- **Federal Teletax Information System**, 800-829-4477 TTD, 800-829-4059 (for recorded federal tax information)
- **Internal Revenue Service**, 316 N. Robert St., St. Paul, 644-7515 (for live help on federal taxes)

To get Minnesota state income tax forms and to ask questions: Call the **Minnesota Department of Revenue**, 10 River Park Plaza, St. Paul, **296-3781**. The forms are also available at libraries and post offices during tax season.

State Property Tax Refunds

Minnesota offers tenants a **renter's property tax refund**. Your landlord is required to send you the Certification of Rent Paid (CRP) form no later than January 31st. You then have nearly seven months (till August 15th) to fill out your half—the M1PR form—and send both in to the state for a refund of the portion of your rent that went to property taxes. The refund may amount to only a small check but it's usually worth filing for. The Minnesota Department of Revenue can answer questions about property tax refunds at the same number as above.

ow that you've landed a place to live and opened a checking account, you're probably wondering: what will it take to bring life back to normal? The first thing you'll have to do is have the phone service, electricity, gas, and perhaps cable TV turned on in your name. Set up your utilities a day or two before you move in, so you don't have to stumble around your apartment searching for a flashlight the first night you spend in your new pad. With this book and a phone, you can do most of your setting up from the comfort of a moving box. (You may want to go ahead and find a chair; some of these people ask a lot of questions.) Also included in this section is a list of broadcast media, so you can surf the dials while you're on hold.

Telephone

You may want to do this one first, because the phone company will immediately assign you a phone number that you can then use for all kinds of other setting-up purposes. And, having a phone number makes you feel like you live here! Local phone service in both Minneapolis and St. Paul is provided by U.S. West. The area code for the entire metropolitan area is still 612. The charge for installation of basic service is $16.25. Depending on your credit history, they may also require a deposit of up to $60. If you don't show up in their credit check, good or bad, you won't need a deposit, but you will have to send them a photocopy of your picture identification. U.S. West's number is: 800-244-1111 (TTY: 800-223-3131)

Cellular Phone and Paging Services

Following are the metro area's two cellular service providers, to get you started.

- **ATT (Cellular One)**, 800-462-4463
- **Air Touch Cellular**, 800-626-6611

Here are some well-known pager suppliers:

- **American Paging**, 672-9828
- **ATT (Cellular One)**, 800-305-9494
- **General Communications (GenCom)**, 920-3455
- **MinnComm**, 522-3344
- **Pagenet**, 884-4400
- **Skytel**, 800-858-4338

Electricity

The supplier of electricity in both Minneapolis and St. Paul is Northern States Power (NSP). Some outlying suburbs have different providers; call the suburb's municipal office number listed in the "Neighborhoods" chapter of this book to find out more. NSP can set you up with a few days' notice, but they recommend two weeks. No deposit is required though NSP charges $10 plus tax for processing, which will appear on your first bill. NSP's telephone number is: 800-622-4677 (TTY: 800-288-5533).

Gas

It's likely that as a new tenant you will have to be set up for gas service (unless it's included in your rent), probably for your furnace, hot water heater and possibly your stove. In St. Paul and adjacent suburbs, the gas supplier is the same as for electricity—NSP (one phone call does it all!). In Minneapolis and adjacent suburbs, it's Minnegasco. Minnegasco charges no deposit or transfer fee, but they'll ask the usual questions. The numbers to call:

St. Paul

- **Northern States Power (NSP)**, 800-622-4677
- **TTY**, 800-288-5533

Minneapolis

- **Minnegasco**, 372-4727
- **TTY**, 321-4997

Water

Water service will probably not be something you'll have take care of when renting. However, if something goes wrong with your water supply, you may call these numbers:

Minneapolis

- **24-hour water emergency**, 673-5600
- **General information**, 673-1114

St. Paul

- **24-hour water emergency**, 298-6888
- **General information**, 266-6350

Consumer Complaints-Utilities

Obviously, try to resolve any billing or other disputes with your phone, gas or electric company on your own first. If a problem persists, however, the people to call are the officials at the **Minnesota Public Utilities Commission**. Their consumer affairs office telephone number is **296-0406**.

Garbage and Recycling

In Minneapolis, the city hauls residential garbage and provides trash containers for each house. Haulers will take one or two large items, such as discarded furniture, per pickup. In Minneapolis, if you've got more garbage than your trash container will hold, just make sure it's bagged and tied, and the haulers will probably take it.

In St. Paul, each household must hire a garbage service (the landlord may already have made arrangements). Your rate will depend on the company you hire and volume of the trash container you choose. City officials believe this system cuts down on waste, and it does get you to root out those recyclables in order to reduce your load. Disposal of large objects must be arranged separately with your hauler. One 30-gallon container for weekly pick-up costs from $10 to $16 per month. You can get a list of available garbage haulers at the number below.

Both Minneapolis and St. Paul have curbside recycling programs that are among the most comprehensive in the nation. For specific information about what's recycled, how to pack it, and when to put it out, call the numbers below. For recycling or garbage pickup information outside of the cities, call the municipal information number listed for each community in the "Surrounding Communities" section of the "Neighborhoods" chapter.

- **Minneapolis Garbage and Recycling**, 673-2917
- **St. Paul Garbage**, 633-3279
- **St. Paul Recycling**, 644-7678

Driver's License, Photo Identification

If you have a valid driver's license from another state, or one that's been expired for less than a year, you can obtain a Minnesota license by passing a written test and an eye exam (no driving test required). Bring your current driver's license and another form of I.D., such as a passport or birth certificate. If you changed your name when you got married, bring your marriage certificate as well. The cost is $18.50.

The Minnesota Department of Public Safety has a substation (listed below) that handles only written and eye exams, and it's centrally located. If you've got a license from another state, it's the place to go. If you need to start from scratch, with a driving test, you will need to go to one of the full testing stations also listed below.

If you're not a driver and are only looking for a state picture I.D., you can also get one at the University Ave. substation. The cost is $12.50; bring one form of identification, such as a passport or birth certificate.

Minnesota Department of Public Safety   296-6911
(general driver license information)

Written Test Substation
Spruce Tree Center   642-0808
1600 University Ave. W., St. Paul
(8 a.m.–6:30 p.m.)

Full Exam Stations
North Metro, Hwy. 8 & W. Co. Rd. I, Arden Hills   639-4057
South Metro, 2070 Cliff Rd., Eagan   688-1870
West Metro, 2455 Fernbrook Ln. N., Plymouth   341-7149

Auto Registration

You have 60 days from the time you move here to register your car with the state of Minnesota. After two months you can be hit with a fine, so it pays to get this done as quickly as possible. Bring your car's certificate of title, insurance information, and your personal identification. The registration tax depends on the value of your car; it will be no less than $35 and could be more than $200 a year (ouch!). Once you're registered, you should receive an annual renewal notice several weeks before your registration expires.

Vehicles in the seven-county metro area also need to pass an **emissions test** as part of their auto registration. This modest act of civic responsibility usually takes no more than a minute or two and can be completed at any of several metro-area testing stations The registration application will include a list of emissions testing stations. If your car is a recent model or if it's older and you keep it tuned up and in good shape, you should pass easily; otherwise you might need to make some repairs. Add your completed emissions test documentation to your registration form. Following are the numbers to call for information on auto registration.

• **Minnesota Department of Public Safety**, 296-6911
• **Hennepin County** (Minneapolis), 348-8241
• **Ramsey County** (St. Paul) , 296-6013

Parking Permits, Stickers, Ramps

Downtown Minneapolis is a beehive of activity—it's the commercial hub of the upper Midwest—so parking is always tight. The city operates 15 ramps, nine lots, and thousands of street meters. If you're planning on commuting into downtown every day, consider purchasing a monthly ramp pass, which costs $100 to $135 a month. All downtown St. Paul ramps are privately owned, but they also offer monthly deals. Call to find the best offer.

It is useful to know that in both cities there are certain areas that are designated **Critical Parking Areas**. Residents in these areas can buy stickers that permit them to ignore the parking restrictions on their streets. Stickers cost $10 a year. For more information on Critical Parking Areas, call the **Division of Public Works** at **673-2411**.

- **Minneapolis Parking Information**, 673-2411
- **St. Paul Parking Information**, 266-6200

Snow Emergency Parking

Winter in Minneapolis-St. Paul means snow (as well as cold), and the arrival of more than a few inches of winter's frozen precipitation brings another peculiar aspect of life in the North: the "snow emergency." So that snowplow crews can do their job, snow emergency rules require that you move your car from one side of the street to the other. Snow emergencies may be called off after plowing is finished or they may remain in place if more snow is forecast. To find out if snow parking rules have been designated, call the relevant snow emergency number below (or tune in to **WCCO-AM Radio** or **Cable TV Channel 34**).

Minneapolis and St. Paul have slightly different snow emergency parking rules. They are as follows:

Minneapolis

- **Night one of a Snow Emergency:** parking is prohibited on both sides of Snow Emergency Routes (streets with blue signs) from 9 p.m. to 8 a.m. These are the city's largest thoroughfares. You can still park on all other streets on this first night.

- **Day two:** parking is prohibited on the odd side of residential streets (green or brown signs) and both sides of parkways (the roads encircling parks) from 8 a.m. to 8 p.m. After 8 p.m., parking returns to normal on Snow Emergency Routes (blue street signs). You can move your car back to the odd side of a residential street.

- **Day three:** parking is prohibited on the even side of residential streets (green or brown signs) from 8 a.m. to 8 p.m.

After 8 p.m. on the third day, parking returns to normal, unless a further snow emergency is deemed necessary. Authorities may call a complete ban on odd-side parking for any amount of time through April 1. Such a ban is always well-publicized. Keep in mind that the parking police follow plows and ticket those cars parked illegally.

St. Paul (watch for "Night Plow Route" signs.)

• **Night one of Snow Emergency**: between 9 p.m. and 6 a.m., streets marked with "Night Plow Route" signs will be plowed. The city's busiest streets, along with one side of north-south residential streets, usually have these signs posted. Watch out for them.

• **Day two:** beginning at 8 a.m., east-west residential streets will be plowed, as well the side of north-south streets not marked with "Night Plow Route" signs.

As in Minneapolis, St. Paul city officials are sticklers about these rules. Avoid a fine and park where they say.

Below are the numbers to call for parking information related to snow emergencies.

• **Minneapolis Snow Emergency Information**, 348-SNOW
• **St. Paul Snow Emergency Information**, 266-PLOW

Towing and Stolen Cars

Ugh! Hope you never need these numbers. The **Minneapolis Impound Lot** is at 51 Colfax Avenue North. Call **673-5777** (have your license plate number ready). To report a stolen car in Minneapolis, call 673-5743. The **St. Paul Impound Lot** is at 830 Barge Channel Road. Their number is **291-9630**. To report a stolen car in St. Paul, call the police department's general number at **291-1111**.

Voter Registration

Naturally, you'll want to join in Minnesota's colorful political tradition by voting. You must be a U.S. citizen, 18 years old and have lived here 20 days before an election. In an effort to get out the vote, registering has been made easier: now you can register when you apply for your driver's license as well as at a county courthouse. Or, if you forget to register in advance, you can just go to the polling station on election day and register there. Bring a driver's license, mail that shows your current address, or a neighbor who can vouch for your residency. You need not register a party affiliation, and primaries are open.

You'll notice references in the news to the "DFL" and the "IR" which are the Democratic Farmer-Labor and Independent Republican Parties. These aren't upstart third parties, they're the state's Democrats and Republicans. The DFL was formed in the 1940s, when Minnesota's Democrats (led by Hubert Humphrey) merged with the populist Farmer-Labor Party. At about the same time, Minnesota's Republicans added "Independent" to their name in the hope of attracting more independent voters. Following are the numbers to call for voter registration information:

- **Hennepin County Voter Registration**, 348-5151
- **Ramsey County Voter Registration**, 266-2171
- **DFL State Office**, 293-1200
- **IR State Office**, 222-0022

Library Cards

Minnesota has always been proud of its investment in education, and it's been ambitious in the funding of libraries. Minneapolis and St. Paul have separate library systems, but they're connected in the following ways: once you get a card at one library system, you can use it to get a card at the other one; you can search for a book and have it delivered from one system to the other; and you can even check out a book from one system and return it to the other. Both systems are online, so you can scan for titles, place requests, and check your borrowing records from home. To get a card, though, you still need to visit a library in person with identification and a piece of mail with your new address (if you don't have a Minnesota driver's license yet). Check the "Neighborhoods" chapter of this book for the library nearest you. Call the following libraries if you have questions.

- **Minneapolis Central Public Library**, 300 Nicollet Mall, 372-6500

- **St. Paul Central Public Library**, 90 W. 4th St., 292-6311,
  New cards, 292-6203

Passports

Passports are processed at county government centers located in each city. Both Hennepin (Minneapolis) and Ramsey (St. Paul) Counties offer convenient systems to take your photo and process your passport at the same time. They're listed below. You need to bring $65 for a new passport ($55 to renew), an extra $7.50 if you need a photo, your birth certificate, photo identification, your social security number, and your parents' birthplaces and dates. A few suburban locations process passports as well; if you have questions call the numbers below.

Minneapolis

- **Hennepin County Government Center**, 300 S. 6th St., 348-8241,
  (Monday–Friday, 8 a.m.–4:30 p.m.)

St. Paul

• **Ramsey County Vital Service Office**, City Hall, 15 W. Kellogg Blvd., Rm. 110, 266-8265, (Monday–Friday, 8 a.m.–4 p.m.)

Cable TV Service

It's a fact, getting settled for most people now includes setting up cable TV service. Minneapolis and St. Paul are served by two separate companies while a host of other cable providers have divvied up the suburban market. In either city, to get cable you'll have to contact the following providers. (To get suburban cable information, call the suburb's general information number listed at the end of the "Neighborhoods" chapter of this book.) Since each cable company has been granted a monopoly by city government, we've included each city's consumer contact number for cable service complaints.

Minneapolis

• **Paragon Cable**, 801 Plymouth Ave. N., 522-2000

St. Paul

• **Continental Cablevision**, 214 E. 4th St., 222-3333

Consumer Complaints about Cable TV
• **Minneapolis Office of Client Services**, 673-2910
• **St. Paul Office of Communications**, 266-8870

TV Stations

For old-fashioned broadcast (free) TV, the Twin Cities offer the national networks, plus independents and a few newcomers, such as Warner Brothers and Paramount Network. Of course, if you've ordered cable the channels will differ from those given here.

Channel 2	KTCA-TV	PBS
Channel 4	WCCO-TV	CBS
Channel 5	KSTP-TV	ABC
Channel 9	KMSP-TV	Paramount
Channel 11	KARE-TV	NBC
Channel 17	KTCI-TV	PBS
Channel 23	KLGT-TV	Warner Brothers
Channel 29	KITN-TV	Fox
Channel 41	KXLI-TV	Independent

Radio Stations

No need to set anything up here—except to twirl your radio dial. Here's a brief guide to what's available on the radio airwaves in the Twin Cities.

Adult Contemporary
KTCJ .... 690 AM
KSTP... 94.5 FM
KTCZ... 97.1 FM
KCFE .... 105.7 FM

Alternative Rock
KUOM .... 770 AM
KEGE .... 93.7 FM, 980 AM
KREV, WREV .... 105.1, 105.3 FM

Big Band
KLBB...................................... 1400 AM, 1470 AM

Black Community News, Music
KMOJ .... 89.9 FM

Children's Programming
WWTC... 1280 AM

Christian, Religious
KTIS .... 900 AM, 98.5 FM
KYCR.. 1570 AM
WCTS .... 1030 AM
KNOF .... 95.3 FM
KKCM .... 1530 AM

Classic, New Rock
KQRS....................................... 92.5 FM, 1440 AM

Classical, National Public Radio News
KSJN... 99.5 FM
WCAL .... 89.3 FM

Community Talk, Eclectic Music
KFAI... 90.3, 106.7 FM

Country
WIXK .... 1590 AM, 107.1 FM
WLKX .... 95.9 FM
WBOB.. 100.3 FM
KEEY .... 102.1 FM
KJJO .... 104.1 FM

Easy Listening
WLTE . . . . 102.9 FM

Jazz, Government Meetings
KBEM . . . . 88.5 FM

National Public Radio News, Talk
KNOW . . . . 91.1 FM, 1330 AM

News, Talk
WCCO . . . . 830 AM
KSTP . . . . 1500 AM

Oldies
KQQL . . . . 107.9 FM
WMIN . . . . 740 AM
WIMN . . . . 1220 AM
KDWA . . . . 1460 AM

Pop, Top 40s
KDWB . . . . 101.3 FM

Sports
WCCO . . . . 830 AM
KFAN . . . . 1130 AM

Safety

First, the (very) good news: when you look at the number of violent crimes reported in the Twin Cities, you can see why Minneapolis-St. Paul residents talk about the great quality of life here. The FBI reports that the metro area typically experiences less than a fourth as many violent crimes as other cities of the same size. Perhaps more significantly, few of these crimes appear to be stranger-on-stranger crimes (although that's not true for less serious acts such as theft). Now the (not so) bad news: according to recent surveys published in the *Star Tribune,* fear of crime now ranks as the number one concern for Twin Cities residents. Having said that, the feeling of safety is different for each person. It's important to trust your instincts, not numbers. Don't forget, though, that you've moved to Minnesota, a place that's still well behind the ever more violent times of the rest of the country.

The police suggest taking the following steps for you to feel safe in your new home:

• Experience your new neighborhood. Talk with your neighbors, local businesses, and others.

• Contact the neighborhood association (see the "Neighborhoods" chapter) and learn about the concerns of neighborhood residents.

- In Minneapolis, if you'd like safety/security information before you choose a neighborhood, you can call the city's Neighborhood Ambassador Program at 673-2491. Volunteers there can tell you in some detail what it's like to live in your neighborhood.

- Prevent! Both cities offer programs on personal safety and methods of avoiding crime on the street. Police volunteers will explain simple and inexpensive ways to secure your home. Find out (at the numbers below) if there is a block or apartment club you can join. If there isn't one, consider volunteering to start one. Police help block clubs resolve problems such as drug houses, noise at night, abandoned property or other potentially difficult situations.

Minneapolis
- **Community Crime Prevention/SAFE**, 217 S. 3rd St., 673-3015

St. Paul
- **FORCE Unit (Community Resources)**, 100 E. 11th St., 292-3712

Finally, if you travel for your job, a useful handbook for those on the go is ***Smart Business Travel: How to Stay Safe When You're On the Road*** by Stacey Ravel Abarbanel.

Perhaps the hardest thing about moving to a new city is not knowing. For instance, after going clear across town for months to get some service or other, you learn there's a better (cheaper!) provider right in your neighborhood. With nicer people! Knowing where to go for a specific service is particularly important when you first move and you're trying to accomplish a dozen things at the same time. The following information should help in your transition. These are some of the first services you may need to call when you've arrived in the Twin Cities.

Day care and Baby-sitting

As a newcomer, it may be particularly difficult to find daycare or baby-sitters because you may not have a wide circle of acquaintances in your new city yet. If possible, ask the local residents you do know and trust about their child care (obviously, the best way to find a good daycare provider is by referral from a friend). There are also two well-known referral services—the **Greater Minneapolis Day Care Association (GMDCA)** and the **Adult and Children's Alliance (ACA)**—which can help find openings at state-licensed providers in the metro area according to your criteria. Both services can find full-time or drop-in service, at any size facility and with any type of activity program. The GMDCA has a sliding-scale fee, while the ACA provides free referrals.

Once you've got a few day care providers in mind, you'll want to visit them—preferably unannounced. In general, three things to look for are safety, cleanliness and a caring attitude on the part of the daycare providers. To that end, look to see that the kitchen, toys and furniture are clean and safe. Ask for the telephone numbers of other parents who use the service and talk to them. Also, ask to see the schedule of a typical day, and make sure it includes both active and quiet time, appropriate for your child's age. In this part of the country, four to five months of the year are spent indoors so you should ask about active time in the winter. Keep in mind that, although the referral services may only list state-licensed child care providers, a license alone does not guarantee a service of the quality you may be seeking. Above all, follow your instincts: if something does not feel right about an individual or a place, keep looking.

If you're only looking for part-time child care, or if the daycare service of your choice has a waiting list, try searching out a regular baby-sitter. A co-worker's teenage son or daughter, or a reliable college student with experience may fit your bill. Several baby-sitting cooperatives also exist in the area. The following services can refer you to them or help you find other daycare possibilities.

- **Greater Minneapolis Daycare Association**, 1628 Elliot Ave. S., Minneapolis, 341-1177

- **Adult and Children's Alliance**, 2885 Country Dr., St. Paul, 481-9320

School Information

If your child will soon be of school age, you may want to do a bit of research since Twin Cities public schools offer open enrollment. This means that you are not limited to sending your children to the school nearest to your house but may enroll them in any public school throughout the city, each of which offers different specializations and teaching formats. For instance, your child may have an aptitude for or an interest in science or languages or your child could have "special needs." You should investigate all available options before selecting a school.

To begin, call your school district to receive information about the offerings of each school. Do not hesitate to talk to your neighborhood organization, friends, and co-workers about this important question.

Although over 80% of all Twin Cities children of school age attend public schools you may choose to forego public schools altogether if you have from $3,000 to $10,000 a year available for tuition at a private school. A variety of private schools offer individualized instruction, many kinds of specialized programs, and impressive facilities. Acquainting yourself with the range of available private schools may seem daunting, but you can start by calling for a copy of *Schoolhouse Magazine*, a periodical that lists and describes the best schools and most innovative programs (public as well as private) in the Twin Cities. A copy costs $4.95 plus tax, and can be obtained by calling **227-1519**.

No matter which type of school you're looking for, another resource you may want to try is **School Match, Inc.**, a firm that keeps records on public and private schools, including student-teacher ratios, test scores and other information. They'll fax you independent reports on schools in which you're interested. The cost for a basic "snapshot" report is $19, and for $97.50, School Match formulates comparisons between different schools in their "Full Search Service." Finally, an organization that will help you to get oriented in your new role, both in terms of advice and support, is the **Minnesota Parent-Teacher Association**, whose number is listed below.

- **Minnesota Parent-Teacher Association**, 631-1736
- **Minneapolis School District**, 627-2050
- **St. Paul School District**, 293-5120
- **School Match, Inc.**, 800-992-5323

Rental Services

In your move, perhaps you streamlined your worldly possessions down to the bare essentials or perhaps you have most of your stuff packed . . . but it's not all here yet. Not to worry, get off that cardboard box and call the following rental services; they'll be more than happy to provide all the comforts of home, for a fee of course. You can find other such businesses in the Yellow Pages; as with all lists in this guide, inclusion here does not mean endorsement. Those listed here are some of the largest or locally owned or both.

Furniture

Bring a list of what you need and if possible a floor plan drawing; staff at the showroom will help you temporarily furnish your new pad.

- **Cort Furniture Rental**, 920 2nd Ave. S., Minneapolis (downtown), 375-1866; 8920 Lyndale Ave. S., Bloomington, 884-5622
- **General Furniture Leasing**, 2575 University Ave. W., St. Paul, 647-4270; 9157 Lyndale Ave. S., Bloomington, 888-7100
- **Home Furniture Rental**, 318 E. Lake St., Minneapolis, 824-7777; 1159 University Ave., St. Paul, 646-4000
- **Quality Furniture Rental**, 916 Rice St., St. Paul, 487-2191; 9125 Lyndale Ave. S., Bloomington, 884-4741

Television, VCR, Stereo

Most of the furniture rental places offer TVs, VCRs, and stereos as well, but you may want to lease from an electronics specialist.

- **Curtis Mathes Showroom**, I-35W at New Brighton Blvd., Minneapolis, 788-9268
- **Robert Paul TV**, 1789 N. Lexington Ave., Roseville, 489-8025

Personal Computers

The places listed here will rent to individuals on a daily, weekly and monthly basis, and they deliver.

- **BMS Computer Rentals**, 944-8838
- **Computer Rental Systems**, 867-6388

- **GE Capital Computer Rental**, 938-1100
- **Houlihan Office Systems**, 338-5354
- **PCR Computer Rentals**, 646-0771

House Cleaning Services

In addition to taking care of routine chores on a regular basis, most cleaning services also offer one-time service; they can give your place a once-over after moving day (or on any occasion, such as after your house-warming party). Check the Yellow Pages for additional services.

- **Cottage Care**, 944-8020
- **Dustbusters**, 288-9486
- **Handy People Inc.**, 636-2105
- **Housecare Extraordinaire**, 724-2664

Mail Receiving Services

When you're in between addresses but you still need a place to receive mail, you can rent a box at the post office. Of course, the friendly, old USPS can have waiting lists not to mention hours that may not fit your busy schedule. Instead, you may opt for a private receiving service. Most such services also allow you to do a call-in mail check or have your mail forwarded, although they are usually much more expensive than a box at the post office.

- **Mailboxes Etc.**, 40 locations metro-wide, 623-4000
- **Postal Service Plus**, Inc., 3208 West Lake St., Minneapolis, 922-4414
- **Mail Bag Etc.**, 2028-B Ford Pkwy., St. Paul, 690-0020

Moving and Storage

Consult the Yellow Pages for leads on moving companies; there are dozens of businesses that provide these services in the Twin Cities. If you've had a problem, the consumer number to call depends on if your move was within Minnesota or across state lines. The state regulates in-state moves, while interstate moving companies are regulated at the federal level. Both agencies and their telephone numbers are listed below.

The story on storage warehouses is essentially the same—there are more of them in the Twin Cities than you can shake a roll of packing tape at. Start with the Yellow Pages listings and call and compare. Storage warehouses tend to be concentrated in current or former industrial areas such as the Midway in St. Paul and Hiawatha Avenue in Minneapolis. The Minnesota Attorney General's consumer division handles complaints about public storage warehouses (see below).

- **Minnesota Department of Transportation**, Office of Motor Carrier Services, 296-7109 (for in-state moving)

- **U.S. Department of Transportation**, Bureau of Motor Carrier Safety , 290-3260 (local call)

Helpful Consumer Protection Numbers

If you've got a consumer complaint about a business transaction in Minnesota there are both public and private resources you can use to get help. Following are government agencies and private nonprofits that assist consumers in the metro area.

- **Better Business Bureau of Minnesota**, 2709 Gannon Rd., St. Paul, 699-1111

- **Federal Consumer Product Safety Office**, 316 N. Robert St., St. Paul, 290-3781

- **Minnesota Attorney General**, Consumer Division, State Capitol Bldg., St. Paul, 296-3353

- **MN Public Interest Research Group** (MPIRG), 2512 Delaware St. SE, Minneapolis, 627-4035

Moving to a new place means running lots of errands in search of something-you-all-of-a-sudden-realize-you-need-right-now-but-don't-have (or can't find in your boxes). To help you through this fun but demanding time of shopping for your new home we offer you this guide to Twin Cities shopping.

As you probably know, the main attraction for many metro residents (and visitors from around the world) is the Mall of America (see below for location and telephone number) which has the distinction, other than its size—five times the area of Moscow's Red Square, seven times the volume of Yankee Stadium—of having brought many well-known retail names to the Twin Cities. Visit this mother of all malls if only to stroll through Underwater World, the 70,000 square-foot aquarium or to try out Legoland or to ride the indoor roller coaster at Camp Snoopy, sure-fire cures for shopping burnout.

Shopping options in the metro area are plentiful and varied since the Twin Cities are second only to Chicago as a center of commerce in the Midwest. If you're accustomed to belligerent big-city "customer service," you'll be pleasantly surprised at how friendly and helpful clerks and salespeople can be in the Twin Cities.

Partly because of the long, severe winters and partly because of the massive urban sprawl and resultant car culture here, indoor malls dominate retail shopping in the Twin Cities. Southdale, just west of Minneapolis, was the first indoor retail center built in the United States. There are dozens more now and the list below will help guide you. But in no way are malls the whole story. Many different shopping districts thrive, some even offer free fresh air to their customers.

Malls

Most of the following malls have a mix of practical and pricey shopping, except for the **Galleria, Gaviidae Common** and the **Conservatory**, which consist mainly of specialty stores and boutiques. In a category of its own is the **Mall of America**, at Highways 77 & I-494 in Bloomington. Its anchor stores are Bloomingdale's, Macy's, Nordstrom's and Sears, but you can find hundreds of other stores for housewares, electronics, and other moving-in needs. The Mall of America can be reached at 883-8800.

- **Apache Plaza**, 38 NE Ave. & Silver Lake Rd., St. Anthony, 788-1666
- **Bandana Square**, 1021 E. Bandana Blvd., St. Paul, 642-9676
- **Calhoun Square**, Hennepin Ave. & Lake St., Minneapolis, 824-1240
- **City Center**, 7th St. & Nicollet Mall, Minneapolis, 372-1200
- **Conservatory**, 8th St. & Nicollet Mall, Minneapolis, 332-4649
- **Galleria**, 3510 Galleria, Edina, 925-9534
- **Galtier Plaza**, 175 E. 5th St., St. Paul, 297-6734
- **Gaviidae Common**, 6th St. & Nicollet Mall, Minneapolis, 372-1222
- **Har-Mar Mall**, 2100 N. Snelling Ave., Roseville, 631-0340
- **Maplewood Mall**, I-694 & White Bear Ave., St. Paul, 770-5020
- **Rosedale**, Hwy. 36 & Fairview Ave., Roseville, 633-0872
- **Signal Hills**, Robert St. & Butler Ave., West St. Paul, 457-0589
- **Southdale**, 6601 France Ave. S., Edina, 925-7885
- **Stadium Village**, 825 Washington Ave. SE, Minneapolis, 331-1822
- **World Trade Center**, 30 E. 7th St., St. Paul, 291-1715

Shopping Districts

The following Twin Cities retail districts offer a variety of useful and one-of-a-kind stores. Besides possessing great moving-in shopping, they also offer many opportunities to get a bite or a cappuccino.

Uptown, Hennepin Avenue at Lake Street, Minneapolis. This is the Twin Cities' best-known commercial district. Besides numerous cafes and bars, many useful houseware, furniture, and home decorating stores exist here. Lake Street, East of Hennepin, gravitates more toward discount and warehouse stores, with a concentration of such stores where Lake meets I-35W.

Grand Avenue, St. Paul. Perhaps the second best-known retail area in the Twin Cities, Grand offers numerous resources for the newcomer, both affordable and high end.

Nicollet Mall, Minneapolis. The city's renowned downtown pedestrian mall includes several national and local housewares and home furnishings stores.

Dinkytown, 10th Avenue to 17th Avenue SE, west of U of M campus, Minneapolis. This area offers a variety of somewhat bohemian, mostly affordable shops.

Linden Hills, 43rd Street and Upton Avenue S., Minneapolis. Offers several first-rate, locally-owned furniture, houseware and antique shops.

50th St. and France Avenue, Edina. Includes Centennial Lakes Plaza indoor mall; offers numerous national chains, some high-end boutiques.

Midway, University Avenue at Snelling Ave., St. Paul. Warehouse and discount department stores, second-hand furniture and clothing retailers.

South Robert Street, West St. Paul. Well-known national department stores, discount stores, housewares, and electronics.

Department Stores

If you have trouble breathing at the thought of living without Blooming-dale's or Nordstrom or some other top of the line department store, you can breathe easier: most of the national one-stop shopping giants are here ready to make your life in the Twin Cities a bit easier. When in Rome, though, don't forget to try out the local favorite: Dayton's (they're the same people who own the popular discount store, Target).

- **Bloomingdale's**, Mall of America, Bloomington, 883-2500
- **Dayton's**, 700 Nicollet Mall, Minneapolis, 375-2200
  (check the Yellow Pages for other locations)
- **Macy's**, Mall of America, Bloomington, 888-3333
- **Neiman-Marcus**, 505 Nicollet Mall, Minneapolis, 339-2600
- **Nordstrom**, Mall of America, Bloomington, 883-2121
- **Saks Fifth Avenue**, 655 Nicollet Mall, Minneapolis, 333-7200
- **Sears, Roebuck & Co.**, Mall of America, Bloomington, 853-0500;
  425 Rice St., St. Paul, 291-4330 (check the Yellow Pages for
  other locations)

Discount Stores

Also, you may want to check out the so-called "factory outlet" stores in malls. Though it's no longer clear that they offer lower prices than else-where, it is clear that they are popular.

- **Filene's Basement**, Mall of America, Bloomington, 858-8514
- **K-Mart**, 10 W. Lake St., Minneapolis, 827-5491
  (check the Yellow Pages for other locations)
- **Nordic Ware Factory Outlet Store**, Hwy. 7 and 100, St. Louis Park,
  924-9672
- **Nordstrom's Only Deals**, 1655 W. Cty. Rd. B2, Roseville, 636-
  3610; 7150 Valley Creek Plaza, Woodbury, 735-4342; 17 Signal
  Hills Center, West St. Paul, 457-5002
- **Sam's Club**, 3745 Louisiana Ave. S, St. Louis Park, 924-9450
  (check the Yellow Pages for other locations)
- **Target,** 1300 University Ave. W, St. Paul, 642-1146
  (check the Yellow Pages for other locations)
- **TJ Maxx**, IDS Center, Nicollet Mall, Minneapolis, 321-9107
  (check the Yellow Pages for other locations)
- **Wal-Mart**, 715 E. 78th St., Bloomington, 854-5600
  (check the Yellow Pages for other locations)

Electronics

- **Audio King**, 7435 France Ave. S., Centennial Lakes Plaza, Edina, 920-4272 (check the Yellow Pages for other locations)
- **Best Buy**, 1300 W. Lake St., Minneapolis, 827-1741; 1647 W. Cty. Rd B2, Roseville, 636-6456 (check the Yellow Pages for other locations)
- **Circuit City**, 1750 W. Hwy. 36, Roseville, 636-2505; Southdale Mall, Edina, 832-5200

Computers

Try the Yellow Pages for computer dealer listings, including specialized dealers who also provide training. Don't forget the larger electronics vendors some of whom have become competitive in computer sales as well as in stereos, compact discs, and the highest resolution television technology. Then there are the ubiquitous mail-order catalogs, such as MacWarehouse, from which you can shop without leaving that warm spot on your couch. Just remember, though, that catalog computer merchants may not be able to offer the same level of post-sale service that a regular retailer does. A few well-known computer hardware makers, such as Zeos, build their product in the Twin Cities, making them convenient for service.

If you're on tight budget or don't need the very latest technology, try one of the following **used computer vendors**:

- **Computer Renaissance, Inc.**, 1305 W. Lake St., Minneapolis, 825-3007; 2335 Fairview Ave., Roseville, 638-9808
- **Used Computer Bank**, 2500 Hwy. 88, St. Anthony, 789-6910

Furniture

- **Danish Woodworks**, 2303 E. Kennedy St., Minneapolis, 378-0954
- **Depth of Field**, 405 Cedar Ave. S., Minneapolis, 339-6061; 917 Grand Ave., St. Paul, 222-5356
- **Elements,** 2941 Hennepin Ave., Minneapolis, 824-5300; 1655 W. Cty. Rd. B2, Roseville, 633-3515; 2940 W. 66th St., Richfield, 866-0631
- **Grandbois Woodworks**, 3130 Excelsior Blvd., Minneapolis, 929-3250
- **Pinecraft**, 261 Water St., Excelsior, 474-0830
- **Unpainted Place**, Inc., 1601 Hennepin Ave., Minneapolis, 339-1500; 1654 Rice St., St. Paul, 487-2226

For those on the most modest of budgets, try second-hand stores (see "Second Hand Shopping" in this chapter); for those with cash to spare, head to the breathtaking interior design showrooms at the International Market Square, 275 Market St. in Minneapolis (338-6250).

Beds and Bedding

- **Depth of Field** (see above listing in "Furniture")
- **Futon Gallery**, 2601 Hennepin Ave., Minneapolis, 377-9440; 799 Grand Ave., St. Paul, 227-2644 (check the Yellow Pages for other locations)
- **Mattress Liquidators**, 4335 Excelsior Blvd., St. Louis Park, 922-2552 (check the Yellow Pages for other locations)
- **Scandia Contemporary Interiors**, 3533 W. 70th St., Edina, 920-6675
- **Slumberland Furniture**, 7801 Xerxes Ave. S., Bloomington, 888-6204 (check the Yellow Pages for other locations)
- **The Company Store**, 800-285-3696 (catalog sales of down-filled bedding)

Carpets and Rugs

- **Carpet King**, 773 Cleveland Ave. S., St. Paul, 690-5448 (check the Yellow Pages for other locations)
- **Cyrus Carpets**, 3464 W. 70th St., Edina, 922-6000
- **Gabberts Furniture**, 3501 Galleria, Edina, 927-1550

Lamps and Lighting

- **Citilights**, 1619 Hennepin Ave., Minneapolis, 333-3168
- **Creative Lighting**, I-94 at Snelling Ave., St. Paul, 647-0111
- **Lamp Depot**, Brighton Village Center, I-694 at Silver Lake Rd., New Brighton 332-6626 (check the Yellow Pages for other locations)
- **Michael's Lamp Studio**, 3101 W. 50th St., Minneapolis, 926-9147

Hardware Stores

The first four listings are primarily supply businesses, although they offer size cutting and other services. The rest are old-fashioned hardware service stores, offering hardware with seasoned expertise. Check the Yellow Pages for more hardware stores.

- **Menards** (check the Yellow Pages for locations)
- **Fleet Farm** (check the Yellow Pages for locations)
- **A.H. Bennett Co.**, 900 Glenwood Ave., Minneapolis, 374-3444
- **Grand Avenue Hardware**, 1676 Grand Ave., St. Paul, 698-3826
- **Hardware on Hennepin**, 1246 Hennepin Ave., Minneapolis, 341-3830
- **Home Depot**
  3550 124th Ave., N.W., Coon Rapids, 422-1200
  6701 Boone Ave., N., Brooklyn Park, 535-9780
  5650 N.E. Main St., Fridley, 571-9600

- **Langula Hardware**, 919 S. Robert St., West St. Paul, 457-8899
- **Rex Hardware**, 2601 Lyndale Ave. S., Minneapolis, 872-9299
- **Seven Corners Hardware**, 216 West 7th St., St. Paul, 224-4859

Housewares (General)

- **Crate and Barrel**, 915 Nicollet Mall, Minneapolis, 338-4000; Southdale Center, Edina, 920-2300
- **Pier One**, 1433 W. Lake St., Minneapolis, 825-5367; 733 Grand Ave., St. Paul, 228-1737 (check the Yellow Pages for more locations)
- **Lechters Housewares**, Rosedale Shopping Center, 636-7725; Maplewood Mall, Woodbury, 770-0563

Second Hand Shopping

Expert thrifting is a necessary art for many. Not only can you find just the right end table, or a snappy field jacket, or just about anything else at rock-bottom prices, but you can have a lot of fun along the way. Thrift store shopping can take some effort and the willingness to spend a bit of time slogging through tables of stuff some people might call junk...but when you find a lovely dress or a gem of an antique for $5, you'll know it was worth it. Start with the list below, then check the newspaper for garage and estate sales. Weekend yard sales are as prevalent an image of summer here as the color green.

- **Disabled American Veterans Thrift Store**, 572 University Ave. W., St. Paul, 292-1707
- **Goodwill Industries**, 2116 E. Lake St., Minneapolis, 721-4187; 1425 S. Robert St., West St. Paul, 451-2014 (check the Yellow Pages for other locations)
- **Lula's**, 1587 Selby Ave., St. Paul, 644-4110
- **Ragstock Clothing**, 315 14th Ave. SE, Minneapolis, 331-6064; 1433 W. Lake St., Minneapolis, 823-6690; 1515 University Ave. W., St. Paul, 644-2733
- **Saint Vincent De Paul Thrift Stores**, 1008 Arcade St., St. Paul, 771-0358; 461 West 7th St., St. Paul, 227-1332
- **Salvation Army**, 3740 Nicollet Ave., Minneapolis, 822-1200; 927 Payne Ave., St. Paul, 776-3585 (check the Yellow Pages for other locations)
- **Reachout Thrift Store**, 417 E. Lake St., Minneapolis, 827-5606
- **Steeple People Surplus**, 2004 Lyndale Ave. S., Minneapolis, 871-8305
- **Tatters Clothing**, 2922 Lyndale Ave. S., Minneapolis, 823-5285

Sporting Goods, Bicycles, Ski Equipment

Contrary to what some newcomers might believe, outdoor recreation is a year-round phenomenon in these parts. Many Minnesotans actually look forward to the winter months for the chance to go skiing, skating, snow-boarding, even curling. In October, die-hard cross-country skiers can be seen rolling along parkways on ski simulator wheels training for the first snow. And in the glorious days of summer with the longer northern days, there's lots of time for biking, swimming, fishing, in-line skating, camping, sailing, volleyball...whatever your heart desires. For those in need of gear, we offer the following list of places to start shopping. If you're counting your pennies, remember to shop the season-end sales, and if you're not sure whether you want to buy an expensive item, inquire about renting.

- **Alternative Bike & Board Shop**, 2408 Hennepin Ave. S, Minneapolis, 374-3635
- **Freewheel Bike Shop**, 1812 S. 6th St., Minneapolis, 339-2219
- **Joe's Ski Shop & Sporting Goods**, 935 N. Dale St., St. Paul, 488-5511
- **Midwest Mountaineering**, 309 Cedar Ave. S., Minneapolis, 339-3433
- **Now Sports Cycling & Fitness**, 3045 Hennepin Ave. S., Minneapolis, 827-2838; 75 N. Snelling Ave., St. Paul, 644-2354
- **Play It Again Sports**, 3505 Hennepin Ave. S., Minneapolis, 824-1231; 1669 Grand Ave., St. Paul, 698-3773
- **REI (Recreational Equipment, Inc.)**, 710 W. 98th St., Bloomington, 884-4315; 1995 W. Cty. Rd. B2, Roseville, 635-0211
- **Rolling Soles** (in-line skate rentals), 1700 W. Lake St., Minneapolis, 823-5711
- **Sportmart**, 1750 W. Hwy. 36, Roseville, 638-3000

Winterwear

In the introduction, we warned you about the winter months and the need for warm clothes. We weren't kidding; winters here are no joke. Fortunately, if you arrived without the right winter gear, the following are a few places where you can get the clothes you'll need to stay warm and happy from Thanksgiving well into March. Also, don't forget department stores.

- **Thrifty Outfitter** (discount goods), 309 Cedar Ave. S., Minneapolis, 339-6290
- **Nokomis Shoe Shop** (discount goods), 4950 34th Ave. S., Minneapolis, 724-1406
- **United Stores**, 9721 Lyndale Ave. S., Bloomington, 881-0868; 449 Snelling Ave. N., St. Paul, 646-3544 (check the Yellow Pages for other locations)

Very soon after moving here you are going to have to eat. There are far too many grocery stores to begin to list them, but a few different kinds of markets and other sources, comprising different corners of the mighty retail food pyramid, are worth noting.

Grocery Stores

At one corner of the pyramid are the warehouse food stores, who's gleaming aisles are lined with formidable towers of boxes, cans, and produce. The two main warehouse food stores in the Twin Cities are **Rainbow** and **Cub Foods**. Both are 24-hour enterprises, enabling you to go on late-night shopping sprees. Both chains have bakeries and delis, as well as small health food sections. If it's 2 a.m. and you want a hundred rolls of toilet paper or a six month supply of cat food, these are the places to go. Check the White Pages for the nearest Cub or Rainbow.

Another corner of the Twin Cities retail food pyramid is occupied by the "quality" food stores, offering such amenities as gourmet and imported foods, fresh flowers, specialty meats and seafoods, and clerks who actually bag your groceries. **Lund's, Byerly's, Kowalski's,** and **New Market** are the main players in this category. Each of these enterprises has stores throughout the metro area; check listings for the nearest one.

Food Co-operatives

If your idea of quality is organically grown produce and health foods, try one of the Twin Cities' many grocery cooperatives. Besides offering unsprayed produce and the gamut of "free" foods (wheat-free, meat-free, dairy-free), co-ops sell many foods in bulk, allowing you to get just as much as you need without paying for packaging. Co-ops sell shares and distribute dividends to members, and some allow you to volunteer at the store for a discount on groceries. Following are the grocery co-ops in the metro area:

- **Capitol City Co-op**, 28 W. 10th St., St. Paul, 298-1340
- **Hampden Park Co-op**, 928 Raymond Ave., St. Paul, 646-6686
- **Lakewinds Natural Foods**, 17507 Minnetonka Blvd., Minnetonka, 473-0292
- **Linden Hills Co-op**, 4306 Upton Ave. S., Minneapolis, 922-1159
- **Mississippi Market**, 1810 Randolph St., St. Paul, 690-0507
- **North Country Co-op**, 2129 Riverside Ave., Minneapolis, 338-3110
- **Seward Co-op Grocery & Deli**, 2201 Franklin Ave. E., Minneapolis, 338-2465
- **Valley Natural Foods**, 14015 Grand Ave. S., Burnsville, 892-6661
- **Valley Co-op**, 215 N. William St., Stillwater, 439-0366
- **Wedge Community Co-op**, 2105 Lyndale Ave. S., Minneapolis, 871-3993

In a class of their own are Tao Foods and Whole Foods. **Tao Foods**, at 2200 Hennepin Ave. in Uptown (**377-4630**), is a small shop that concentrates on the boundary between food and medicine, offering homeopathic remedies, herbal tonics and a juice bar. **Whole Foods**, at 30 Fairview Ave. S. in St. Paul (**690-0197**), is a hybrid of the co-ops and gourmet grocery stores, offering organic and health foods, as well as gourmet foods and a bakery, in a supermarket-style venue. Be advised, though: Whole Foods is not a place to shop for bargains.

Farmers' Markets

If you're shopping for the highest quality in fruits and vegetables, nothing beats buying directly from the growers. Summers are bountiful here, producing scores of farmers' markets throughout the metro area. Following are a few of the best and largest markets to be found. Don't forget: this is farm country, and there are many more farm markets around. If a drive in the country with a stop to pick fresh raspberries or apples sounds like a cure for your city blues, get the full listing of farm stands in Minnesota from this address: **Minnesota Grown**, Minnesota Department of Agriculture, 90 West Plato Blvd., St. Paul, Minnesota, 55107 (or call 297-8695).

- **Minneapolis Farmers' Market**, 333-1718, Exit 230 from I-94: Daily, 6 a.m. to 1 p.m., Apr. 24 to Dec. 24. Nicollet Mall: Thursdays, 6 a.m. to 6 p.m., May to November. Minnesota's largest open-air market. Fresh produce, fish, meats, bedding plants, maple syrup, wreaths and trees before Christmas.

- **St. Paul Farmers' Market**, 227-6856, 290 E. Fifth St. (Lowertown), Saturdays, 6 a.m. to 1 p.m., Apr. 29 to Nov. 4. Sundays, 8 a.m. to 1 p.m., May 6 to Oct. 30. Wednesdays, 2 to 5 p.m., July 12 to Sept. 13. Fresh produce, honey, eggs, fresh-cut flowers, plants, trout, buffalo meat, Hmong handiwork.

- **Afton Apple Orchards**, 436-8385, 14421 S. 90th St., Afton. Daily, 8 a.m. to 6 p.m. (or until picked out), June to July. Daily, 10 a.m. to 6 p.m., August to October. Pick up or pick your own strawberries, raspberries, apples and pumpkins. Call ahead for harvest information. Also, honey, preserves, maple syrup, cider, and hayrides in the fall.

- **Berry Brook Farm**, 424-8700,10311 Noble Ave. N., Brooklyn Park 8 a.m. to Noon, 5 to 7:30 p.m., Tue.–Sat., Noon to 4 p.m. Sun (in season) Pick your own strawberries, blueberries, raspberries; roadstand.

- **Peterson Produce**, 972-2052, Hwy. 12 at I-394, Delano. Daily, 10 a.m. to 6 p.m., beginning in May. Pick your own fresh asparagus, raspberries, pumpkins and more; farm stand including sweet corn, tomatoes, broccoli, herbs, honey, squash.

- **Hawk's View Farm**, 507-645-8282, Dakota County. Rd. 23 just south of County. Rd. 86. Daily except Sunday, 10 a.m. to 6 p.m., May to November. Organically grown produce, you-pick peas, cut flowers, squash, pumpkins.

Ethnic Markets

Groceries specializing in cuisine from a particular part of the world are scattered throughout the Twin Cities. Below are some of the best places to go for specific ethnic foods, although this is by no means a complete list.

African (Sub-Saharan)

- **Merkato African Groceries**, 605 Cedar Ave. S., Minneapolis, 673-0308

Greek-Middle Eastern

- **Bill's Imported Foods**, 721 W. Lake St., Minneapolis, 827-2891
- **Holy Land Bakery & Deli**, 2513 Central Ave. NE, Minneapolis, 781-2627

Italian

- **Broder's Cucina Italiana**, 2308 W. 50th St., Minneapolis, 925-3113
- **Buon Giorno Italian Market**, 335 University Ave. E., St. Paul, 224-1816
- **Cossetta's**, 211 W. 7th St., St. Paul, 222-3476

Latino-Mexican

- **El Burrito Mercado**, 175 Concord St., St. Paul, 227-2192
- **Las Americas**, 401 E. Lake St., Minneapolis, 827-3377

East Asian (including Chinese, Lao, Vietnamese, and Thai)

University Ave. east of Lexington in St. Paul is lined with dozens of Asian grocery stores. Also, try the 500 to 1600 blocks on Rice Street. In Minneapolis, go to Nicollet Ave. between 24th and 27th Streets. The following shops are good places to start:

- **Asia Import Food & Video**, 1840 Central Ave. NE, Minneapolis, 788-4571
- **Midway Oriental Food & Video**, 512 Snelling Ave. N., St. Paul, 645-3619
- **Phil's Oriental Foods**, 789 University Ave. W., St. Paul, 292-1325

Scandinavian–Eastern European

- **Ingebretson's**, 1601 E. Lake St., Minneapolis, 729-9331
- **Kramarczuk Sausage Co.,** 215 Hennepin Ave. E., Minneapolis, 379-3018
- **Surdyk's**, E. Hennepin Ave. & University Ave. NE, Minneapolis, 379-9757

Drinking Water

Twin Cities tap water is not as bad as in many other urban communities in the U.S.; still increasing numbers of people here have become concerned about the quality of their municipal tap water. As a result sales of bottled drinking water (which may or may not, depending on the supplier, be any better than tap water) have soared. There a number of high-quality drinking water delivery services, and they rent coolers as well. Also, artesian water taps in St. Paul are supplied for free by two local breweries. Of course, that means you must do your own lugging and driving. They're listed below. An increasingly popular option is a water purifier for your tap water. Check the Yellow Pages for suppliers.

Drinking Water Services

- **Chippewa Springs**, Ltd., 2125 Broadway NE, Minneapolis, 379-4141
- **Glenwood Inglewood Co.**, 225 Thomas Ave. N., Minneapolis, 374-2253
- **Great Glacier, Inc.**, Princeton, 333-6944
- **Kandiyohi Bottled Water Co.**, Willmar, 566-1566

Self-Serve Artesian Wells

- **Minnesota Brewing Co.** (April to November), 882 W. 7th St., St. Paul, 228-9173
- **Stroh Brewery Co.** (year-round), 707 Minnehaha Ave. E., St. Paul, 778-3100

Other Food Resources

For the ultimate in freshness, you need to grow your own. It doesn't take much space; a window box will do for herbs or tomatoes. Many neighborhoods also have community gardens—check with your neighborhood organization for possibilities.

A local farm cooperative offers another way to get your vegetables fresh as can be. **The Land Stewardship Project** runs a community supported agriculture program that can set you up with organically grown produce over an entire season for a one-time fee. Service, which varies from farm to farm, generally includes organically grown produce, drop-off service within city limits, and a split share option which is good for smaller families or individuals. You may also be able to participate in events at the farms where the produce is grown, including hayrides, festivals and chore weekends. For more information:

- **Land Stewardship Project**, 2200 4th St., White Bear Lake, 653-0618

Besides snow, the quality of health care is probably one of the most reliable features of living in Minnesota. Compared to other states, Minnesota has a high number of community clinics, a high rate of immunizations, and a low infant mortality rate. Life expectancy here is nearly 78. That's second only to Hawaii, without the benefit of a warm, tranquil climate.

No one knows for sure why Minnesotans are so long-lived but perhaps it has something to with the great tradition of medical innovation in the state. The Mayo Clinic, in nearby Rochester, needs no introduction, nor does the University of Minnesota Hospital in the Twin Cities, which is known for, among other things, its transplant research. There has been innovation on the insurance side, too. The concept of health maintenance organizations, or HMOs, began here. And in 1992, the state legislature passed a health-care reform bill that controls medical costs and offers a subsidized insurance plan to low-income residents.

Insurance

The state insurance plan is called **MinnesotaCare**. It is funded by a 2% tax on doctor services, some federal money, and by the modest premiums that users pay for the plan. It is administered by the state Department of Human Services. To qualify, you must be a Minnesota resident for six months, have no coverage from any other health plan, and have no access to employer-paid health insurance. Also, your income must be below federally-set guidelines ($10,452 for a single adult, $13,980 for couples, $28,488 for a single parent with child, $35,700 for a couple with child). MinnesotaCare's information number is **297-3862**. For those with more resources, the following are traditional health insurance options:

Employer- or school-provided insurance - Dollar for dollar this is probably your best option, if it's available. Of course, the degree of coverage varies from one plan to another, but without a doubt an employer or other institution can get a better rate than any individual. Overwhelmingly, employer plans today are handled by **HMOs** or **managed-care systems**, companies that handle all of your health care through one group of doctors. One negative: these "primary physicians" must usually receive approval from corporate managers to do any expensive procedures or to refer you to a specialist.

Blue Cross and Blue Shield of Minnesota - This corporation is the best-known insurance provider for individuals. A practical option if you can't get coverage through your employer, Blue Cross is also good if you're on the move and don't plan to stay with your present employer for long because your coverage will stay with you. Blue Cross offers the traditional **deductible** insurance, which means you pay up to your deductible amount per year and over that amount the insurer pays the majority of the costs. You choose your doctor from a directory that includes most local physicians. Contact Blue Cross/Blue Shield of Minnesota at the following number: **800-531-6685**.

Other individual coverage - If you've been living well and you don't expect to bear children or incur other significant health costs anytime soon, consider getting very basic deductible coverage from an insurance company. Your auto insurance provider or agent may offer low-cost, low-coverage health insurance to protect you against an unexpected catastrophe.

Clinics

If you're strapped for cash while in transition, following are a few tips that will keep you healthy for less:

The University of Minnesota Dental Clinics - The U provides inexpensive dentistry services as part of their instruction program. An initial visit costs $21, with x-rays: $35. Fillings are filled for $30-$75 and they do surgery if necessary. There are minor negatives—your appointments may last as long as three hours, and you may have to return more often than you're used to—but the service is excellent. Students are typically diligent and attentive, and instructors hover around them. Where else can you get second and third opinions on procedures while you wait? The clinic is in the U of M's Moos Tower, 515 Delaware St. SE, Minneapolis. Their number is **624-8400**.

Community Clinics - If you don't mind an occasional wait, these non-profit clinics offer the best deal for routine visits such as physicals or minor health problems.

- **Cedar-Riverside People's Center**, 2000 S. 5th St., Minneapolis, 332-4973
- **Central Avenue Clinic**, 2610 Central Ave. NE, Minneapolis, 781-6816
- **Family Medical Center**, 5 W. Lake St., Minneapolis, 827-9800

- **Fremont Clinic**, 3300 Fremont Ave. N., Minneapolis, 588-9411
- **Hennepin Care North**, 6601 Shingle Creek Pkwy., Brooklyn Center, 569-3737
- **Hennepin County Medical Center**, 701 Park Ave., Minneapolis, 347-2121
- **Pilot City Health Center**, 1313 Penn Ave. N., Minneapolis, 520-8877
- **St. Paul Public Health Center**, 555 Cedar St., St. Paul, 292-7727
- **Sheridan Women's and Children's Clinic**, 342 13th Ave. NE, Minneapolis, 362-4111
- **Southside Community Clinic**, 4243 4th Ave. S., Minneapolis, 822-3186
- **West Side Health Center**, 153 Concord St., St. Paul, 222-1816
- **Women & Children's Health Center**, 810 1st St. S., #220, Hopkins, 569-2660

Resources for the Handicapped

The slogan for a disabled advocacy program on KFAI, a local community radio station, is "Disabled and Proud—Not an Oxymoron!" This slogan could also describe the supportive environment for the handicapped in the Twin Cities. Here the physically challenged will find visibility (a reporter for one of the local TV stations works from a wheelchair), organization, communication, and reliable mobility. Since the passage of the federal Americans with Disabilities Act in 1990, Twin Cities institutions have taken seriously the mandate to provide complete access for all. The number of programs for the physically, visually, and hearing-impaired continues to increase throughout the metro area. Below are numbers to call for specific information.

Getting Around

- **Metro Mobility** - The transportation system for the physically handicapped throughout the metropolitan area. It's a call-for-pickup service. Fares are $2.50 during rush hour (6–9 a.m. and 3:30 to 6:30 p.m.) and $2 for other times. You can buy ten-ride books for convenience, although there's no discount on them. Call at least a day in advance or as much as two weeks ahead.

- **Metro Mobility** (Reservations and Information), 221-0015

- **Bus Service** - Bus lines with wheelchair access are marked on maps and schedules. Wheelchair lifts are not provided on a large number of routes but they are available on the main arteries, including the #16 on University Avenue and many express lines. For the visually impaired, the driver is trained to be helpful. When the bus stops, the driver announces the route number of the bus to the person waiting if they're carrying a walking stick. Also, the driver will help the passenger get on if he or she appears to need assistance. Call for schedules or a map.

- **Metropolitan Council Transit Operations**
  General information, 373-3333
  TTY (hearing-impaired) information, 341-0140
  TTY Customer Relations, 349-7439

- **Cars** - If you need to get "Handicapped" plates and stickers, call the state Department of Transportation (DOT) at the number below. Also listed is the DOT's telephone number for road conditions.

- **Minnesota Department of Transportation**
  "Handicapped" license and stickers, 296-6911
  "Handicapped" license and stickers (TTY), 297-2100
  Road conditions, 296-3076
  Road conditions (TTY), 296-9930

Communication

The telephone system for the hearing- and speech-impaired is called **Minnesota Relay Service (MRS),** and it's administered by a private company under contract with the state. "Communications assistants," assist you with your calls. MRS is available 24 hours a day, 365 days a year and there are no restrictions on the length or number of calls you are permitted to place. All calls are guaranteed to be confidential, and no records of call contents are kept. To use Relay, you'll need the right equipment. The state's **Regional Service Center for Deaf and Hard of Hearing People** can refer you to companies that sell the keyboard and other equipment you will need in order to use Relay. The center can also give you equipment on permanent loan (if you qualify as low-income), set you up with amplifiers, message lights, and other helpful equipment. You'll see both TDD (telecommunications device for the deaf) and TTY (telecommunications typing) listings for many numbers—TDD is essentially a new name for the same system. Call the following numbers:

- **Minnesota Relay Service**
  To place a call in the metro area, 297-5353
  To place a call out of state, 800-627-3529
  Information in voice, 800-657-3788
  Information in TTY, 800-657-3789
  Customer service (TTY/voice), 800-676-3777

- **Regional Service Center for Deaf/ Hard of Hearing People**
  Voice, 297-1316
  TTY, 297-1313

Other Resources for the Handicapped

Following is a variety of resources, both governmental and non-profit, that may be of use to those with special needs in the Twin Cities.

- **Accessible Space**, 2550 University Ave. W., #330N, St. Paul, 645-7271. Locates disability-adaptive housing and support.

- **ARC Minnesota,** Provides a wide variety of support for people with disabilities. Call the nearest office.
  Hennepin County Office, 4301 Hwy. 7 #40, Minneapolis, 920-0855
  Anoka and Ramsey County Office, 425 Etna St., #36, St. Paul, 778-1414
  Minnesota Office, 3225 Lyndale Ave. S., Minneapolis, 827-5641

- **Descriptive Video Service**, 800-333-1203
  (films for visually impaired viewers)

- **Epilepsy Foundation**, 800-779-0777

- **Hennepin County Services for Persons with Disabilities**
  Voice, 348-3440
  TTY, 879-3218

- **Metropolitan Center for Independent Living**, 646-8342

- **Minnesota State Council on Disability**, 296-6785

- **Minnesota Health Care Administration**,296-7675
  (for information about coverage),

- **Ramsey County Human Services**
  Voice, 266-4444
  TTY, 266-3750
  (for general information and financial assistance)

- **Vision Loss Resources, Inc.**, 871-2222

A final note: "Disabled and Proud" airs on Tuesday nights at 7:30 on **KFAI**, 90.3 FM in Minneapolis and 106.7 FM in St. Paul.

For most newcomers to the Minneapolis-St. Paul area, particularly those from warm climes, the most common concern is the allegedly fearsome winter. There is no denying (if you've ever looked at Minnesota on a national weather map from mid-November through mid-March you'll know it's true) that Minnesota gets hit with bitter cold weather systems that dip south from Canada blanketing the winter-time Twin Cities in sub-zero temperatures and deep snow. In fact, in January it's not unusual to have a weeklong period of sub-zero (that's sub-zero, not sub-freezing) temperatures, or for April to bring a blizzard (eight to ten inches of snow is the monthly wintertime average). But having a real winter means one can easily enjoy outdoor activities, such as skiing and ice-fishing, that residents of other places must hop on a plane to enjoy. Of course, living through the long winters gives residents a keen appreciation for the verdant radiance of summer. And summers here are sunny, often hot, and oh-so-green, a welcome tonic to the cold days of winter. Also, in contrast to boring places like balmy southern California, because the weather here seems to change almost every day there's always something to talk about with a stranger. Finally, where did the notion start that a mono-climate is better than a varied one, anyway? Three cheers for Minnesota seasons!

Lest we get carried away, though, winters in the Twin Cities can take some getting used to, and we hope that the following information will help you make the adjustment as quickly and painlessly as possible.

Driving

First of all, although it sounds obvious, it is important to remember that driving is slower and more dangerous in the cold months. If the forecast includes bad road conditions, give yourself 15-30 minutes extra time to get to your destination including at least five minutes to warm up your car. If you are taking the bus, you may want to take an earlier connection than you might otherwise; along with the rest of the traffic buses move more slowly, and they could be running behind schedule.

Before winter really kicks in (before Thanksgiving, that is), take the following steps to winterize your vehicle. Change the radiator fluid and switch to a lighter oil (more viscous at low temperatures). Consider buying snow tires and an engine block heater (the origin of the electrical cords you see hanging out of the grilles of some cars). These devices run a low electrical current through your engine to keep it warm overnight. They're particularly helpful if you don't have a garage, although you may find it impractical to run an extension cord out to your car. Finally, think about the age of your battery. If it's getting a bit grizzled, replace it with a new one. On those crackly January mornings when it's 20 degrees below zero and you stick your key in the ignition, begging and swearing may not turn your engine over but that new battery will.

Next, stash the following useful items somewhere inside your car:

- A set of jumper cables, for yourself or for the neighbor stranded on the road.
- A bag of sand and a small snow shovel, to help dig your way out of a wipeout (car mats work for tire traction, too).
- A "stranded" emergency kit, consisting of several blankets, a candle in a coffee can (a makeshift heater), matches, a flashlight (with batteries that work), and a couple of candybars.

Once the Arctic weather has arrived, keep your gas tank from getting near empty—the water content of the fuel will actually freeze in the gas lines preventing any fuel from getting to the engine. Also, keep in mind that in cold weather high-octane fuel runs better than low-octane.

If you've never driven in snowy conditions before, try driving someplace out of harm's way first, such as in a parking lot, before venturing out onto the streets. Practice easing on the brakes to avoid losing control on ice. The trick to maintaining control when you start to "fishtail" (when the back wheels slide out to the left or right as you hit the brakes) is to steer into the direction that your back wheels are sliding. Try it, it works. *Above all, drive as slowly as conditions demand.*

As mentioned, you will have to leave a little extra time to drive anywhere. Many drivers make an extra key for their car, so they can go out, start up their vehicle, lock it, and return to get ready while the inside of the car gets nice and warm. The police however, counsel against doing this, because of the easy (and warm!) target you leave for a car thief. To be safe, you can sit inside the car as it warms up. Just remember your hat and mittens. If your car is off the street or nearby, though, warming it up as you wait indoors is quite an amenity on a cold morning. On particularly cold nights, start your car up for ten minutes or so before going to bed; it gives your engine and battery an extra charge for the morning.

For specific rules on winter parking, see the heading "Parking" in the "Getting Settled" chapter.

Did we remember to tell you to drive slowly?

Insulation

Since this guide concentrates mostly on those who are renting, it will not delve into the details of home insulation. If you are interested in heating efficiency, plenty of helpful resources exist. In Minneapolis, start with the **Center for Energy and Environment**, at **335-5828**. In St. Paul, call the **St. Paul Neighborhood Energy Consortium** at **644-5436**. If there's a drafty window you'd like to fix, a trip to the hardware store ought to do you. An ingenious product now available is clear sheet plastic for your window that contracts with heat. After sizing the sheet over the window, attach it to the frame using double-sided tape. Then, using a hair dryer, heat the plastic until it becomes taut. This should keep drafts out for the rest of the winter. In the spring, when the tulips start pushing out of the ground and you crave fresh air, the plastic easily detaches.

Apparel

As we suggested in the introduction to this Newcomer's Handbook, you should get a heavy coat (down-lined is warmest). Snow boots will reduce your chances of suffering a major wipeout on the sidewalk, not to mention frozen toes. A down quilt gives immeasurable pleasure during sub-zero nights. All of these supplies can be had from sources listed under the heading "Winterwear" in the "Shopping for the Home" chapter. Don't worry about looking clunky—everybody's doing it. If you have to wear more formal shoes at work, or if you just don't like to lug heavy boots around on your feet all day, consider leaving a pair of light shoes at work. Remember: there's no sales tax on clothing in the gopher state!

Pleasure and Recreation

If you haven't realized it by now, life does not stop dead between November and March. Midwesterners, from the native Americans of yesteryear to the residents of today, have found ways to live through and actually enjoy the winter. After the first freeze, new life emerges at the parks. Casual circles of skaters glide across the lakes. Parents watch their kids slip and slide around hockey rinks. Cross-country skiers shuffle across hill and dale. Small groups huddle over holes in the ice, waiting for the big one. To learn more about what activities are available in the parks, read the "Parks and Greenbelt" chapter of this book.

Of course, winter is a perfect time for snuggling and other indoor activities. There are plenty of inclement nights to read a book, watch a video, start that novel you've been meaning to write, teach yourself Latin, learn to play the ukulele, work on your situps, veg out in front of the Home Shopping Network, create new recipes . . . or just curl up, alone or with a friend. The bitter temperatures outside give particular satisfaction to these simple pleasures.

If you need to get out of the house, but you'd rather stay indoors, consider joining a health club or the YMCA (see the "Sports and Recreation" chapter). You may also want to work off your cabin fever at the cavernous **Metrodome**. Home to the baseball Twins and football Vikings, the Dome hosts running and in-line skating nights throughout the winter as well as events such as the Kids' Winter Warm-Up, where children are permitted to roam free on the Dome's playing field and watch entertainment programs. For information, call **335-3370**.

There are an infinite number of ways to stay happy and avoid what the medical profession has diagnosed as Seasonal Affective Disorder, or in non-clinical terms, the winter blues. Nonetheless, five months is a long stretch of time to live with freezing temperatures and scant sunlight. Always remember that winter will end, and the robins will return. And don't forget, it doesn't cost much to hop on a plane to Mexico!

Despite their well-deserved reputations as Lutheran centers, the Twin Cities contain houses of worship from nearly every faith on earth. Obviously there are too many active houses of worship in Minneapolis and St. Paul to list here but we offer the following as a place to start.

African Methodist Episcopal

- **St. James AME Church**, 3600 Snelling Ave., St. Paul, 721-4566
- **St. Peters AME Church**, 401 E. 41st St., Minneapolis, 825-9750
- **Wayman AME Church**, 1221 7th Ave. N., Minneapolis, 374-4711

Apostolic

- **Rehoboth Church of Jesus Christ**, 916 31st Ave. N., Minneapolis, 529-2234

Assemblies of God

- **Bethel Assemblies of God**, Nicollet Ave. & 57th St., Minneapolis, 866-3227
- **Bloomington Assemblies of God**, 8600 Bloomington Ave. S., Bloomington, 854-1100
- **Summit Avenue Assembly of God**, 854 Summit Ave., St. Paul, 228-0811
- **Roseville Assembly of God**, 2353 N. Chatsworth, Roseville, 484-6018

Baha'i

- **Baha'i Faith**, 200 17th Ave. N., Hopkins, 935-5636

Baptist

- **Bethany Baptist Church**, Skillman & Cleveland Ave., St. Paul, 631-0211
- **Bethesda Baptist Church**, 1118 S. 8th St., Minneapolis, 332-5904
- **First Baptist Church**, 10th & Hennepin Ave., Minneapolis, 332-3651
- **First Baptist of White Bear**, Hwy. 61 at Buffalo St., White Bear Lake, 429-9227

Buddhist

- **Karma Kagyu Minneapolis**, 4301 Morningside Rd., Edina, 926-5048
- **Minnesota Zen Meditation Center**, 3343 E. Lake Calhoun Pkwy., Minneapolis, 822-5313
- **Soka Gakkai International USA**, 1381 Eustis St., St. Paul, 645-3133

Catholic

- **Basilica of St. Mary**, 88 N. 17th St., Minneapolis, 333-1381
- **Cathedral of St. Paul**, 239 Selby Ave., St. Paul, 228-1766
- **Liberal Catholic Church of St. Francis**, 3201 Pleasant Ave., Minneapolis, 823-4276
- **Presentation of the Blessed Virgin Mary**, Larpenteur Ave. at Kennard St., St. Paul, 777-8116
- **St. Albert the Great Church**, 2836 33rd Ave. S., Minneapolis, 724-3643
- **St. Olaf Catholic Church**, 215 S. 8th St., Minneapolis, 332-7471
- **St. Stephens Catholic Church**, 2211 Clinton Ave. S., Minneapolis, 874-0311

For more information: **Archdiocese of St. Paul and Minneapolis**, Chancery, 226 Summit Ave., St. Paul, 291-4400.

Christian Science

- **First Church of Christ,** Scientist, 739 Summit Ave., St. Paul, 224-9915
- **Second Church of Christ,** Scientist, 228 S. 12th St., Minneapolis, 332-3368
- **Third Church of Christ**, Scientist, 42nd St. & Xerxes Ave. S., Minneapolis, 926-3511

Church of Christ

•**Minneapolis Central Church of Christ**, 1922 4th Ave. N., Minneapolis, 374-5481
•**Summit Avenue Church of Christ**, 10 S. Grotto, St. Paul, 222-0872

Congregational

• **First Congregational Church of Minnesota**, 500 8th Ave. SE, Minneapolis, 331-3816
• **Colonial Church**, 6200 Colonial Way, Edina, 925-2711
• **Plymouth Congregational Church**, 1900 Nicollet Ave., Minneapolis, 871-7400
• **Woodbury Community Church**, 2975 Pioneer Dr., Woodbury, 739-1427

Disciples of Christ

• **Bloomington Christian Church**, I-35W & 90th St. W, Bloomington, 888-4933
• **First Christian Church**, 2201 First Ave. S., Minneapolis, 870-1868
• **Park Christian Church**, 700 Summit Ave., St. Paul Park, 459-1098

Eastern Orthodox

• **Russian Orthodox Church of Resurrection**, 1201 Hathaway Ln. NE, Fridley, 574-1001
• **St. George Greek Orthodox Church**, 1111 Summit Ave., St. Paul, 222-6220
• **St. Mary's Orthodox Cathedral**, 1701 NE 5th St., Minneapolis, 781-7667
• **Ukrainian Orthodox Church of St. George**, 316 4th Ave. SE, Minneapolis, 379-1647

Episcopal

• **Anglican Church of St. Dunstan**, 4241 Brookside Ave. S., St. Louis Park, 920-9122
• **Cathedral Church of St. Mark**, 519 Oak Grove St., Minneapolis, 870-7800
• **Messiah Episcopal Church**, 1631 Ford Pkwy., St. Paul, 698-2590
• **St. Paul's Church on the Hill**, 1524 Summit Ave., St. Paul, 698-0371
• **St. Paul's Episcopal Church**, 1917 Logan Ave. S., Minneapolis, 377-1273

Evangelical

- **First Covenant Church**, 810 S. 7th St., Minneapolis, 332-8093
- **Grace Church of Roseville**, 1310 W. Cty. Rd. B2, Roseville, 633-6479
- **First Evangelical Free Church of Minneapolis**, 5150 Chicago Ave. S., Minneapolis, 827-4705

Friends (Quakers)

- **Minneapolis Friends Meeting**, 4401 York Ave. S., Minneapolis, 926-6159
- **Twin Cities Friends Meeting**, 1725 Grand Ave., St. Paul, 699-6995

Hindu

- **Geeta Ashram Church**, 10537 Noble Ave. N., Brooklyn Park, 493-4229
- **Hindu Mandir**, 1835 NE Polk Ave., Minneapolis, 788-1751

Independent/Interdenominational

- **Church Upon the Rock**, 7901 NE Red Oak Dr., Minneapolis, 786-9555
- **Evergreen Community Church**, 1300 W 106th St., Bloomington, 887-1646
- **Japanese Fellowship Church**, 4217 Bloomington Ave., Minneapolis, 722-8314
- **Living Waters Christian Church**, 1002 2nd St. NE, Hopkins, 938-4176
- **Spiritual Life Church**, 6500 Shingle Creek Pkwy., Brooklyn Center, 560-7221

Islamic

- **Islamic Center of Minnesota**, 1401 Gardena Ave. NE, Fridley, 571-5604

Jehovah's Witnesses

- **Lake Harriet Congregation**, (with Spanish), 3715 Chicago Ave. S., Minneapolis, 825-6312
- **Lake of the Isles Congregation**, 701 Humboldt Ave. N., Minneapolis, 374-2793

- **Como Park Congregation**, 270 Wheelock Pkwy., St. Paul, 489-8925
- **Riverview Congregation**, (with Spanish), 1545 Christensen Ave., West St. Paul, 457-7139

Jewish-Conservative

- **Adath Jeshurun Congregation**, 1109 Zane Ave. N., Golden Valley, 545-2424
- **Beth El Synagogue**, 5224 W. 26th St., St. Louis Park, 920-3512
- **Sharei Chesed Congregation**, 2734 Rhode Island Ave. S., St. Louis Park, 929-2595
- **Temple of Aaron Congregation**, 616 S. Mississippi River Blvd., St. Paul, 698-8874

Jewish-Reform

- **Mount Zion Temple**, 1300 Summit Ave., St. Paul, 698-3881
- **Temple Israel**, 2324 Emerson Ave. S., Minneapolis, 377-8680

Jewish-Orthodox

- **Lubavitch House**, 15 Montcalm Ct., St. Paul, 698-3858

Lutheran

- **Calvary Lutheran Church**, 7520 Golden Valley Rd., Golden Valley, 545-5659
- **Central Lutheran Church**, 333 S. 12th St., Minneapolis, 870-4416
- **Como Park Lutheran Church**, 1376 W. Hoyt Ave., St. Paul, 646-7127
- **Gloria Dei Lutheran Church**, 700 Snelling Ave. S., St. Paul, 699-1378
- **Hmong Community Lutheran Church**, 301 Fuller Ave., St. Paul, 293-1279
- **Holy Trinity Lutheran Church**, 2730 E. 31st St., Minneapolis, 729-8358
- **Latvian Evangelical Lutheran Church**, 3152 17th Ave. S., Minneapolis, 722-4622
- **Lutheran Campus Ministry of U of M**, 317 17th Ave. SE, Minneapolis, 331-3552
- **Mt. Olivet Lutheran Church**, 5025 Knox Ave. S., Minneapolis, 926-7651
- **St. John's Lutheran Church**, 49th & Nicollet, Minneapolis, 827-4406

- **Shephard of the Hills Lutheran Church**, 500 Blake Rd., Edina, 935-3457

For more information on Lutheran churches, contact the **Evangelical Lutheran Church Association** at 870-3610 (Minneapolis) or 224-4313 (St. Paul).

Meditation Centers

- **Hawkwind Metaphysical Center**, 3525 Hennepin Ave., Minneapolis, 822-4034
- **Meditation Center**, 631 University Ave. NE, Minneapolis, 379-2386
- **Minneapolis Satsang**, 2300 24th Ave. S., Minneapolis, 721-4360
- **Transcendental Meditation Program**, 266 Summit Ave., St. Paul, 641-0925

Mennonite

- **Faith Mennonite Church**, 2720 E. 22nd St., Minneapolis, 375-9483
- **St. Paul Mennonite Fellowship**, 576 S. Robert St., St. Paul, 291-0647

Metaphysical

- **Lake Harriet Community Church**, 4401 Upton Ave. S., Minneapolis, 922-4272

Methodist, United

- **Hamline United Methodist Church**, 1514 Englewood Ave., St. Paul, 645-0667
- **Hennepin Avenue United Methodist Church**, 511 Groveland at Lyndale Ave., Minneapolis, 871-5303
- **Walker Community United Methodist Church**, 3104 16th Ave. S., Minneapolis, 722-6612
- **Wesley United Methodist Church**, Marquette Ave. & Grant St., Minneapolis, 871-3585

Presbyterian (USA)

- **Aldrich Avenue Presbyterian Church**, 3501 Aldrich Ave. S., Minneapolis, 825-2479
- **Bryn Mawr Presbyterian Church**, 420 S. Cedar Lake Rd., Minneapolis, 377-5222
- **Central Presbyterian Church**, 500 Cedar St., St. Paul, 224-4728

- **Christ Presbyterian Church**, 6901 Normandale Rd., Edina, 920-8515
- **Randolph Heights Presbyterian Church**, 435 S. Hamline Ave., St. Paul, 698-3889
- **Westminster Presbyterian Church**, Nicollet Mall & 12th St., Minneapolis, 332-3421

Unitarian

- **First Unitarian Society of Minneapolis**, 900 Mt. Curve Ave., Minneapolis, 377-6608
- **Unity Unitarian Church**, 732 Holly Ave., St. Paul, 228-1456

United Church of Christ

- **All Nations Indian Church**, 1515 E. 23rd St., Minneapolis, 721-4393
- **First Congregational Church of Minnesota**, 500 8th Ave. SE, Minneapolis, 331-3816
- **Mayflower Congregational Church**, 106 E. Diamond Lake Rd., Minneapolis, 824-0761
- **Macalester Plymouth United Church**, 1658 Lincoln Ave., St. Paul, 698-8871
- **St. Paul's United Church of Christ**, 900 Summit Ave., St. Paul, 224-5809

Wesleyan

- **Waite Park Wesleyan Church**, 1510 33rd Ave. NE, Minneapolis, 781-7434
- **Oakdale Wesleyan Church**, 6477 N. 10th St., Oakdale, 739-2940

T win cities boosters always plug the arts and culture here and with good reason. The Walker Art Center is internationally famous for its cutting edge exhibits. The Guthrie Theater is considered one of the best, most interesting theaters in the country. The St. Paul Chamber Orchestra is held in high regard by classical music aficionados everywhere. And popular music acts from Bob Dylan to the Replacements and Paul Westerberg to the man sometimes known as Prince originated in the thriving club scene here. Did we mention the lively colleges and universities, the vibrant literary/coffee house scene or the great casinos?

Music—Symphonic, Choral, Opera, Chamber

They also call this the land of ten thousand standing ovations.

Minnesota Chorale 333-4866
528 Hennepin Ave., #211, Minneapolis
This symphonic chorus of 155 singers performs regularly with the Minnesota Orchestra and the St. Paul Chamber Orchestra.

Minnesota Composers' Forum 228-1407
332 Minnesota St., #E145, St. Paul
Concert series and other forums for emerging composers are the forte of this unique organization.

Minnesota Opera 333-6669
620 N. 1st St., Minneapolis
The Minnesota Opera always brings fresh interpretations to both traditional and contemporary opera.

Minnesota Orchestra 371-5656
Orchestra Hall, 1111 Nicollet Mall, Minneapolis
Conductor Eiji Oue has brought new energy to the Orchestra, which performs evening concerts, midday shows, weekend pops series and at the Viennese Sommerfest, as well as St. Paul's Ordway Theater.

Plymouth Music Series   870-0943
1900 Nicollet Ave., Minneapolis
Founded by Philip Brunelle, the series hosts world-known orchestral and choral performers and assists emerging composers. Their schedule always includes a holiday gala event.

St. Paul Chamber Orchestra   224-4222
75 W. 5th St., St. Paul
This internationally-known 33-player ensemble is the only full-time chamber orchestra in the U.S. It performs at numerous venues in town, but most often at the Ordway Theater in St. Paul. Maestro Hugh Wolff is the musical director, and Bobby McFerrin is creative director. McFerrin also takes up the baton on occasion. For a newcomer's kit that includes two tickets for the price of one, call 291-1144.

Thursday Musical   333-0313
Temple Israel, 24th & Hennepin Ave., Minneapolis
A non-profit partnership that offers inexpensive classical performances by professional musicians.

Music–Contemporary

Maybe it's the long winters with lots of time to practice; for whatever reason, the Twin Cities have a long, rich history of great popular music. From Bob Dylan starting out playing the coffeehouses of Cedar-Riverside, to Prince rocking the house at First Avenue, to garage-rock bands such as the Replacements and Hüsker Dü, the Twin Cities have been and continue to be a place to catch great gigs and perhaps experience music history in the making. The following venues are best-known for the category under which they're listed, although many of them book a variety of acts. Keep in mind that clubs that book popular music are often "here today, gone tomorrow"; our advice is to call first.

Blues, Rhythm & Blues

- **Blues Alley**, 15 N. Glenwood Ave., Minneapolis, 333-1327
- **Blues Saloon**, 601 Western Ave., St. Paul, 228-9959
- **Bunker's**, 761 Washington Ave. N., Minneapolis, 338-8188
- **Cabooze**, 917 Cedar Ave. S, Minneapolis, 338-6425
- **Five Corners Saloon**, 501 Cedar Ave. S., Minneapolis, 338-6424
- **Lyon's Pub on Sixth**, 16 S. 6th St., Minneapolis, 333-6612
- **Nikki's Cafe and Bar**, 107 3rd Ave. N., Minneapolis, 340-9098
- **O'Gara's Garage**, 164 N. Snelling Ave., St. Paul, 644-3333
- **Schuller's Tavern**, 7345 Country Club Dr., Golden Valley, 545-9972
- **Viking Bar**, 1829 Riverside Ave., Minneapolis, 332-4259
- **Whiskey Junction**, 901 Cedar Ave., Minneapolis, 338-9550

Country, Bluegrass

- **Buckboard Saloon**, 464 S. Concorde Exge., South St. Paul, 455-9995
- **Dudley's**, 3020 W. 133rd St., Shakopee, 445-8112
- **Dulono's**, 607 W. Lake St., Minneapolis, 827-1726
- **Gatlin Brothers Music City**, Mall of America, Bloomington, 858-8000
- **Pardner's**, 31 N. Lake, Forest Lake, 464-8686
- **Spring Inn**, 355 Monroe Ave. NE, Minneapolis, 623-0757

Folk, Eclectic

- **Bryant-Lake Bowl**, 810 W. Lake St., Minneapolis, 825-3737
- **Cedar Cultural Centre**, 416 Cedar Ave. S., Minneapolis, 338-2674
- **Chang O'Hara's Bistro**, 498 Selby Ave., St. Paul, 290-2338.
- **Fine Line Music Cafe**, 318 First Ave. N., Minneapolis, 338-8100
- **Ginkgo Coffeehouse**, 721 N. Snelling Ave., St. Paul, 645-2647
- **Kuppernicus Coffeehouse**, 308 Prince St. #421, St. Paul, 290-2718
- **Loring Cafe**, 1624 Harmon Pl., Minneapolis, 332-1617
- **Minneapolis Cafe**, 2730 W. Lake St., Minneapolis, 920-1401
- **New Riverside Cafe**, Cedar at Riverside Ave., Minneapolis, 333-4814

Irish and Celtic

- **Half Time Rec Bar**, 1013 Front St., St. Paul, 488-8245
- **Kieran's Irish Pub**, 330 2nd Ave. S., Minneapolis, 339-4499

Jazz

- **Cafe Luxeford**, 1101 LaSalle Ave., Minneapolis, 332-6800
- **Caffe Solo**, 123 N. Third St., Minneapolis, 332-7108
- **D'Amico Cucina**, 100 N. 6th St., Minneapolis, 338-2401
- **Dakota Bar and Grill**, Bandana Square, St. Paul, 642-1442
- **Jazzville**, 488 N. Robert St., St. Paul, 291-1767
- **Nikolet's**, 815 Nicollet Mall, Minneapolis, 341-4011
- **Times Bar and Cafe**, 1036 Nicollet Mall, Minneapolis, 333-2762

Polka, Lounge Music

- **Bel Rae Ballroom**, 5394 Edgewood Dr., Moundsview, 786-4630
- **Ivories**, 605 Waterford Park Tower, Plymouth, 591-6188
- **Mayslack's**, 1428 4th St. NE, Minneapolis, 789-9862
- **Nye's Polonaise Room**, 112 Hennepin Ave. E., Minneapolis, 379-2021

Reggae, World Beat, Latin

- **Amelia's**, Galtier Plaza, St. Paul, 291-1590
- **Red Sea**, 320 Cedar Ave. S., 333-1644
  (Also see Cedar Cultural Centre)

Rock—Alternative, Eclectic

- **First Avenue**, 701 1st Ave. N., Minneapolis, 332-1775
- **7th Street Entry**, 701 1st Ave. N., Minneapolis, 332-1775
- **Four Hundred Bar**, Cedar at Riverside Ave., Minneapolis, 332-2903
- **Lee's Liquor Bar**, 12th and Glenwood Ave. N., Minneapolis, 338-9491
- **Saloon**, 830 Hennepin Ave., Minneapolis, 332-0835
- **Whole Music Club**, Coffman Union, U of M, 300 Washington Ave. SE, Minneapolis, 624-8638

Rock—Metal, Classic

- **Cat Ballou's**, 12 N. Main St., Stillwater, 439-4567
- **Hexagon Bar**, 2600 27th Ave. S., Minneapolis, 722-3454
- **Iron Horse**, Cty. Rd. 81 & Bass Lake Rd., Crystal, 533-2503
- **Mirage**, 2609 26th Ave. S., Minneapolis, 729-2387
- **Neon's**, 1955 English St., Maplewood, 774-8787
- **Ryan's**, 4th & Sibley St., St. Paul, 298-1917

Nightclubs and Discos

- **Gator's**, Mall of America, Bloomington, 858-8888
- **Gay 90s**, 408 Hennepin Ave., Minneapolis, 333-7755
- **Graffiti's**, 14 N. 5th St., Minneapolis, 333-8820
- **Ground Zero**, 15 NE 4th St., Minneapolis, 378-5115
- **Quest Club**, 110 5th St. N., Minneapolis, 338-3383
- **Terminal Bar**, 409 E. Hennepin Ave., Minneapolis, 623-4545
- **Tropix**, 400 N. 3rd Ave., Minneapolis, 333-1006

Concert Halls, Arenas

- **Guthrie Theater**, 725 Vineland Pl., Minneapolis, 377-2224
- **Hubert H. Humphrey Metrodome**, 900 S. 5th St., Minneapolis, 335-3370
- **Northrop Auditorium**, 84 Church St. SE, Minneapolis, 624-2345
- **Orpheum Theater**, 910 Hennepin Ave. S., Minneapolis, 339-7007
- **Ordway Music Theater**, 345 Washington St., St. Paul, 224-4222
- **O'Shaughnessy Auditorium**, 2004 Randolph Ave., St. Paul, 690-6701
- **St. Paul Civic Center**, 143 W. 4th St., St. Paul, 224-7361
- **Target Center**, 600 N. 1st Ave., Minneapolis, 673-0900

Music–Participatory

Besides lessons, the following places offer classes and open playing sessions.

- **Homestead Pickin' Parlor**, 6625 Penn Ave. S., Richfield, 861-3308. Classes and individual lessons in all folk instruments.
- **MacPhail Center for the Arts**, 1128 LaSalle St., Minneapolis, 321-0100. Music, theater and dance lessons for children and adults.
- **Minneapolis Drum and Dance Center**, 3013 Lyndale Ave. S., Minneapolis, 827-0771. Classes in drumming and ethnic dance.
- **Rymer School of Music**, 2256 Lexington Ave. N., St. Paul, 488-6100. Private lessons for children and adults in all orchestra instruments, as well as voice and acting.
- **West Bank School of Music**, 1813 S. 6th St., Minneapolis, 333-6651. Classes and individual lessons in a variety of musical instruments.

Dance–Performance Groups

Some of the following are cross-listed below as organizations that also offer dance lessons.

- **Ballet Arts Minnesota**, 528 Hennepin Ave., Minneapolis, 340-1071
- **Ballet of the Dolls**, 1620 Harmon Pl., Minneapolis, 333-2792
- **Ethnic Dance Theater**, 2337 Central Ave. NE, Minneapolis, 782-3970
- **Minnesota Dance Theater**, 528 Hennepin Ave., Minneapolis, 338-0627
- **Zenon Dance Company**, 528 Hennepin Ave., Minneapolis, 338-1101

Dance–Participatory and Lessons

- **Arthur Murray School of Dance**, 10 S. 5th St., Minneapolis, 333-3131; 5041 France Ave. S., Edina, 920-1900
- **Ballet Arts Minnesota**, 528 Hennepin Ave., Minneapolis, 340-1071
- **Ballet of the Dolls**, 1620 Harmon Pl., Minneapolis, 333-2792
- **Classical Ballet Academy of Minnesota**, 249 E. 4th St., St. Paul, 290-0513
- **Tapestry Folk Dance Center**, 310 E. 38th St., Minneapolis, 825-3668
- **Zenon Dance Company**, 528 Hennepin Ave., Minneapolis, 338-1101

Theater

Large-scale touring productions, locally-based performance groups, and experimental theater all peacefully coexist here.

- **Chanhassen Dinner Theaters**, 501 W. 78th St., Chanhassen, 934-1525. Lavish stagings of well-known plays in a dinner theater.
- **Children's Theater Company**, 2400 S. 3rd Ave., Minneapolis, 874-0400. A nationally-known company that interprets classical children's plays.
- **Cricket Theater**, 528 Hennepin Ave., Minneapolis, 337-0747. Presents unconventional material by emerging playwrights.
- **Great American History Theater**, 30 E. 10th St., St. Paul, 292-4323. Stages productions relevant to American history, particularly in the Midwest.
- **Guthrie Theater**, 725 Vineland Pl., Minneapolis, 377-2224. A Twin Cities landmark, this repertory theater stages innovative presentations of classical and modern plays.
- **Hey City Stage**, 824 Hennepin Ave., Minneapolis, 333-9202. Polished productions of well-known plays.
- **Illusion Theater**, 528 Hennepin Ave., Minneapolis, 338-8371. A non-profit professional group that writes and produces new plays, with a focus on overcoming interpersonal violence.
- **In the Heart of the Beast Puppet Theater**, 734 E. Lake St., Minneapolis, 721-2535. A troupe that stages spectacular mask-and-oversized-puppet performances, often with a political theme.
- **Jungle Theater**, 709 W. Lake St., Minneapolis, 822-7063. A 100-seat capacity theater that produces intense interpretations of both well-known and obscure plays.
- **Loring Playhouse**, 1633 S. Hennepin Ave., Minneapolis, 332-1617. A professional performance company that has staged new plays and dance performances with an experimental bent.
- **Mixed Blood Theater**, 1500 S. 4th St., Minneapolis, 338-6131. Innovative productions, often with multicultural and racial themes.
- **Old Log Theater**, 5175 Meadville St., Excelsior, 474-5951. Well-established dinner theater, stages comedies and popular plays.
- **Ordway Theater**, 345 Washington St., St. Paul, 224-4222. A lavish space that hosts nationally touring musicals, dance troupes, and concerts.
- **Orpheum and State Theaters**, 910 and 805 Hennepin Ave., Minneapolis, 339-7007. After a city-funded rehab, these two grand theaters provide an opulent setting for touring musicals and concerts.
- **Park Square Theater**, St. Peter St. at Kellogg Blvd., St. Paul, 291-7005. Interpretations of popular plays.
- **Patrick's Cabaret**, 506 E. 24th St., Minneapolis, 222-2738. Performance art and experimental theater weekly.

- **Penumbra Theater Company**, 270 N. Kent St., St. Paul, 224-3180. An acclaimed professional theater company, staging established and new plays with African-American themes.
- **Red Eye Collaborative**, 15 W. 14th St., Minneapolis, 870-0309. Alternative theater and dance, performance art, films.
- **Southern Theater**, 1420 Washington Ave. S., Minneapolis, 340-1725. Alternative productions, dance and performance art.
- **Theatre de la Jeune Lune**, N. 1st St. and N. 1st Ave., Minneapolis, 333-6200. Founded by French and American actors, this group stages ambitious performances in a rehabbed warehouse district building.
- **Theater in the Round**, 245 Cedar Ave., Minneapolis, 333-3010. A community theater that stages the classics as well as new plays.

Casinos

This is definitely participatory entertainment, although you can just go and watch. Currently all casinos in Minnesota are Native American-owned. Most remain open all night.

- **Black Bear Casino**, 601 Hwy. 210, Carlton, 888-771-0777
- **Grand Casino**, Mille Lacs, 800-626-LUCK
- **Grand Casino**, Hinckley, 800-GRAND-21
- **Grand Portage Lodge and Casino**, Box 307, Grand Portage, 800-232-1384
- **Jackpot Junction**, Morton, 800-538-8379
- **Mystic Lake Casino**, Prior Lake, 800-262-7799
- **Treasure Island Casino**, Hwy. 61 and 316, Red Wing, 800-222-7077

Comedy

Some clubs feature comics on certain nights only. Call for schedules.

- **Acme Comedy Co.**, 708 N. 1st St., Minneapolis, 338-6393
- **Bryant-Lake Bowl Show Lounge**, 810 W. Lake St., Minneapolis, 825-8949
- **Comedy Gallery St. Paul,** 175 E. 5th St., St. Paul, 331-JOKE
- **Comedy Olympix**, Limelight Theater, 1414 W. 28th St., Minneapolis, 871-1903
- **Dudley Rigg's Brave New Workshop**, 2605 S. Hennepin Ave., Minneapolis, 332-6620
- **Knuckleheads Comedy Club**, Mall of America, Bloomington, 854-5233
- **The Laughing Cup**, 1819 Nicollet Ave., Minneapolis, 870-7015
- **Stevie Ray's**, 4608 Columbus Ave. S., Minneapolis, 825-1832

Museums–Art

The glimmering Weisman Museum, recently built on the University of Minnesota campus overlooking the Mississippi gorge, is the Twin Cities' latest attraction in visual art. If you want to experience the art scene up close, you should attend smaller gallery openings and shows and bimonthly gallery "crawls"—a night of openings in Minneapolis' and St. Paul's warehouse districts. Call a gallery to find out where and when these fun evenings take place.

Minneapolis Institute of Arts   870-3131
2400 S. 3rd Ave., Minneapolis
This art college houses three floors of galleries and a collection that includes art from a variety of periods and genres. It also hosts traveling exhibits.

Minnesota Museum of American Art   292-4355
Landmark Center, 5th and Market Streets, St. Paul
A museum focusing on the diverse history of American artists. Also offers adult and children's classes.

Walker Art Center   375-7577
Events information line   375-7622
725 Vineland Place, Minneapolis
A Twin Cities landmark, in more ways than one. The permanent collection is world-famous, and the Walker's outdoor sculpture garden is, after the Mall of America, the city's most sought-out place by visitors. The Walker also sponsors classes, off-site performance art shows and summer movies in nearby Loring Park.

Frederick R. Weisman Art Museum   625-9494
333 E. River Rd., University of Minnesota, Minneapolis
Minnesota's newest art museum features an elaborate rigging of polished steel siding, designed by Frank Gehry, which reflects the colors of the sunset and the adjacent Mississippi gorge. The permanent collection consists of contemporary visual art.

Museums–Other

American Swedish Institute   871-4907
2600 Park Ave., Minneapolis
A massive turn-of-the-century stone house shows a permanent collection of Swedish artifacts and hosts traveling exhibits.

Bell Museum of Natural History   624-1852
17th Ave. SE and University Ave., University of Minnesota, Minneapolis
Exhibits, classes and other activities for adults and children with a focus on natural history.

Fort Snelling State Park   725-2390
Hwy. 5 at Hwy. 55, Minneapolis
The first permanent structure built here by European settlers, the fort
overlooks the confluence of the Mississippi and Minnesota Rivers.
Also the site of a massive internment of the Dakota tribe. Costumed
guides perform history demonstrations and give tours.

Minneapolis Planetarium   372-6644
Minneapolis Public Library, 300 Nicollet Mall, Minneapolis
The Planetarium re-creates the night sky each day, and gives a
series of special lectures and presentations.

Minnesota Children's Museum   225-6000
10 W. 7th St., St. Paul
This zany museum fills the senses with colors and shapes, and
offers several permanent galleries, hands-on exhibits, an auditorium,
and classrooms.

Minnesota History Center   296-6126
345 W. Kellogg Blvd., St. Paul
The Center's archive holds correspondence and records of historical
figures, photographs, and maps of properties, among other materi-
als. A genealogy research center, three exhibit galleries and an
excellent cafe are also to be found here. The History Center admin-
isters several historic buildings in the city, such as the James J. Hill
mansion.

Science Museum of Minnesota and Omnitheater   221-9444
10th and Wabasha Streets., St. Paul
The Science Museum is a multi-level extravaganza of hands-on
exhibits and creative demonstrations of physical, biological, environmental science, and more. It also houses the Omnitheater, a 180-
degree view screen showing science-related films.

Zoos, Animal Sanctuaries

Como Zoo   488-5571
Midway Pkwy. and Kaufman Dr., St. Paul
Como Zoo was established at the turn of the century on Harriet
Island (on the river!) before floods forced it to relocate. It's a tradi-
tional zoo, featuring a menagerie of exotic animals.

Minnesota Zoo   432-9000
1300 Zoo Blvd., Apple Valley
This nationally-known zoo houses animals brought from climate
zones around the world similar to Minnesota's. As a result, it's open
year 'round. It also hosts outdoor concerts in the summer.

Raptor Center, University of Minnesota   624-4745920
Fitch Ave., St. Paul
Students and volunteers give tours of this bird hospital. The center also shows off some winged residents and houses a permanent exhibit.

Higher Education

Concerts, lecture series, courses, and many other cultural and educational opportunities are offered by local colleges and universities. Besides the University of Minnesota, the metro area has numerous private, state and community colleges. Call the following numbers or watch campus kiosks for events.

- **Augsburg College**, 731 21st Ave. S., Minneapolis, 330-1000. Set on the West Bank, Augsburg hosts conferences on social issues.
- **Bethel College**, 3900 Bethel Dr., Arden Hills, 638-6400. Bethel is a Baptist college in a quiet suburban setting.
- **College of St. Catherine**, 2004 Randolph Ave., St. Paul, 690-6000; 7601 25th Ave. S., Minneapolis, 690-7700. This Catholic women's four-year college now admits men to its masters programs as well at its two-year technical campus in Minneapolis. St. Catherine hosts concerts, lectures and exhibits.
- **Concordia College**, 275 Syndicate St. N., St. Paul, 641-8211. A private Lutheran college, Concordia sponsors exhibits and lectures.
- **Hamline University**, Hewitt and Snelling Ave., St. Paul, 641-2800. Host of the Putnam lecture series, Hamline offers graduate-level courses with specialization in Humanities.
- **Macalester College**, Grand Ave. at Snelling Ave., St. Paul, 696-6900. A handsome campus with a rising national reputation is known for producing dedicated social activists, Macalester is located among the cafés and bookstores on Grand Ave.
- **Metropolitan State University**, 730 Hennepin Ave., Minneapolis, 341-7250; 700 7th St. E., St. Paul, 772-7777. Founded in 1971, this state-funded commuter school offers, day, evening and weekend classes to more than 8,000 students pursuing vocationally-oriented bachelor's degrees.
- **Minneapolis College of Art and Design**, 2501 Stevens Ave. S., Minneapolis, 874-3700. Undergraduate courses in art and design, touring exhibits, films and lectures are all offered by MCAD.
- **Minneapolis Community College** (MCC), 1501 Hennepin Ave., Minneapolis, 341-7000. Located near downtown on lovely Loring Park, MCC offers associate degrees in dozens of academic areas.
- **Normandale Community College**, 9700 France Ave. S., Bloomington, 832-6320. Non-residential two year community college offering associates degrees to approximately 7,500 students in day and evening classes.

- **University of Minnesota**, Washington Ave. at E. River Rd., Minneapolis; Como Ave. at Cleveland Ave., St. Paul; 625-5000. With an enrollment of over 40,000, "the U" as it is affectionately called is one of the nation's largest universities. Special lecture series are offered by the Humphrey Institute of Public Affairs, 301 19th Ave. S., Minneapolis, 625-9505.
- **University of St. Thomas**, 2115 Summit Ave., St. Paul, 962-5000. A Roman Catholic university of 9,000 students, St. Thomas is the largest private school in Minnesota.
- **William Mitchell College of Law**, 875 Summit Ave., St. Paul, 227-9171. Founded in 1900, this 1100-student private law school is set among the mansions of the attractive Summit Avenue Historic District.

Movies–Art, Revival, Non-Major Releases

The Uptown, the Lagoon, and the Parkway all show new releases that are not bound for the mega-multi-plex at the mall. The U Film Society and Bijou show a combination of new movies and revivals, and the UFS hosts the Rivertown Film Festival, a yearly smorgasbord of hundreds of international films. The Oak Street runs revival series. The others host film screenings as part of other programs. For more commercial fare, check the newspapers and the Yellow Pages for the theater of your choice.

- **American Swedish Institute**, 2600 Park Ave., Minneapolis, 871-4907
- **Bijou**, University of Minnesota (various locations), 626-6930
- **Lagoon Theater**, 1320 Lagoon Ave. S., Minneapolis, 825-6006
- **Minneapolis Institute of Arts**, 2400 3rd Ave. S., Minneapolis, 870-3131
- **Oak Street Cinema**, 309 Oak St., Minneapolis, 331-3134
- **Parkway**, 48th St. and Chicago Ave., Minneapolis, 822-3030
- **Red Eye Collaboration**, 15 W. 14th St., Minneapolis, 870-0309
- **U Film Society**, University of Minnesota, 17th Ave. SE and University Ave., Minneapolis, 627-4430
- **Uptown Theater**, 2906 Hennepin Ave., Minneapolis, 825-6006
- **Walker Art Center**, 725 Vineland Pl., Minneapolis, 375-7622

Readings, Storytelling

Minnesotans love to gather and listen to lectures, poetry and tall tales (this is, after all, the land of Paul Bunyan and Garrison Keillor). The following venues offer stimulating readings and/or lectures as well as a great way to meet like-minded people.

- **Amazon Bookstore**, 1612 Harmon Pl., Minneapolis, 338-6560. Readings by women authors.

- **Barnes and Noble Bookstores**, 3216 W. Lake St., 922-3238; 801 Nicollet Mall, 371-4443. See the Yellow Pages for other locations. Readings, signings and lectures by nationally known authors.
- **Borders Bookshop**, 3001 Hennepin Ave. S., Minneapolis, 825-0336; 1501 Plymouth Rd., Minnetonka, 595-0977. Touring authors read and discuss their work and sign books.
- **Coffee Gallery**, 715 W. Franklin Ave., Minneapolis, 870-9508. Open readings on the third Wednesday of the month.
- **Hungry Mind Bookstore**, 1648 Grand Ave., St. Paul, 699-0587. National and regional writers read and discuss their work at this Twin Cities landmark. Occasionally, readings are held at Weyerhauser Chapel next door. Hungry Mind publishes an excellent quarterly book review.
- **Kuppernicus Coffeehouse**, 308 Prince St., St. Paul, 290-2718. Poetry readings twice a month, on the second and fourth Monday.
- **The Laughing Cup**, 1819 Nicollet Ave., Minneapolis, 870-7015. A comedy venue that hosts open readings on Sundays.
- **The Loft**, Pratt Community Center, 66 Malcolm Ave. SE, Minneapolis, 379-8999. This writer's workshop schedules regular readings by both acclaimed and emerging writers.
- **Once Upon a Crime**, 604 W. 26th St., Minneapolis, 870-3785. Readings by mystery writers for the would-be sleuth in all of us.
- **St. Martin's Table**, 2001 Riverside Ave., Minneapolis, 339-3920. Readings and lectures on social and spiritual issues.
- **Seward Cafe**, 2129 E. Franklin Ave., Minneapolis, 332-1011. Storyteller's stage on Friday evenings.
- **Walker Art Center**, 725 Vineland Pl., Minneapolis, 375-7622. Lectures by visiting artists, readings by authors.

On-Line Services

Day by day, the virtual world of cyberspace becomes more and more grown up with dozens of providers and millions of users. Following is a sample list of area access providers who can offer local features as well as personal help without a busy signal. For more information pick up a free copy of **InfoNation**, which is full of online information, including lists of bulletin boards and an e-mail Yellow Pages. Obtain a copy at a computer store or newsstand, or by writing: 2616 Harriet Ave., #116, Minneapolis, 55408 (http://www.info-nation.com). If you are starting from scratch, the **Science Museum of Minnesota** offers computer classes and information. Call **221-4722**.

- **Bitstream Underground**, 321-9290 (http://www.bitstream.net)
- **Gofast.Net**, Inc., 647-6109 (http://gofast.net)
- **Goldengate Internet Services**, info@goldengate.net

- **Millennium Communications**, 338-5509 (http://www.millcom.com)
- **Minnesota Micronet**, 681-8018 (info@mm.com)
- **MinnNet Communications Inc.**, 944-8660 (info@minn.net)
- **PCLink**, 541-5656 (http://www.pclink.com)

When you're new in town, volunteering for an organization is a satisfying way to help your new community as you get acquainted with it. It's also an excellent way to make new friends with people who care about the same issues that you do. And you can join the great tradition of organized volunteerism in Minnesota. Women at the turn of the century here fought for prison reform, bought and rehabbed buildings, established parent-teacher associations, and of course, helped gain the right to vote. Today Twin Cities service organizations are known for their work in everything from refugee assistance to addiction recovery. Any of them could use a hand, strapped as they typically are for cash. If you've got the urge to volunteer, but don't know one cause from another, try calling these volunteer placement services:

- **United Way of Minneapolis**, 404 S. 8th St., Minneapolis, 340-7400
- **United Way of St. Paul Area**, 166 E. 4th St., St. Paul, 291-8300
- **Volunteers of America**, Minnesota Office, 5905 Golden Valley Rd., Golden Valley, 546-3242

You can find specific volunteer opportunities in newspaper listings, the Yellow Pages, or advertisement postings. Following is a sample of the possibilities, listed by category:

AIDS

- **AIDS Emergency Fund**, P.O. Box 582943, Minneapolis, 331-7733
- **AIDS Project Minnesota**, 1400 S. Park Ave., Minneapolis, 341-2060
- **The Aliveness Project**, 730 E. 38th St., Minneapolis, 822-7946
- **Red Door Clinic**, 525 Portland Ave., Minneapolis, 348-6363
- **Youth & AIDS Projects**, 428 Oak Grove St., Minneapolis, 627-6820

Alcohol and Drug Dependency

- **American Indian Services**, 735 E. Franklin Ave., Minneapolis., 871-2175. Culturally specific transitional treatment.
- **Arrigoni House**, Inc., 508 University Ave. SE, Minneapolis., 331-6582
- **Eden Programs**, 1025 Portland Ave., Minneapolis, 338-0723
- **Hazelden Foundation**, Center City, 257-4010
- **African-American Family Services**, 2616 Nicollet Ave., Minneapolis, 871-7878
- **Park Avenue Center**, 2525 Park Ave., Minneapolis, 871-7443
- **Wayside House**, 3705 Park Center Blvd., St. Louis Park, 926-5626. Treatment and shelter for chemically dependent women.

Children

- **Big Brothers & Big Sisters**: St. Paul, 166 E. 4th St., 224-7651; Minneapolis: 2915 Wayzata Blvd. S., 374-3939
- **Casa de Esperanza**, P.O. Box 75177, St. Paul, 772-1723. Spanish speaking family services.
- **Children's Defense Fund**, 550 Rice St. #205, St. Paul, 227-6121
- **Children's Home Society of Minnesota**, 2230 Como Ave., St. Paul, 646-6393
- **Family and Children's Service**, 414 S. 8th St., Minneapolis, 339-9101
- **Pillsbury House**, 3501 Chicago Ave. S., Minneapolis, 824-0708
- **Sabathani Community Center**, 310 E. 38th St., Minneapolis, 827-5981

Cultural Identity

- **American Indian Business Development Corporation**, 1433 E. Franklin Ave., Minneapolis, 870-7555. Job creation, business help.
- **American Indian Center**, 1530 Franklin Ave. E., Minneapolis, 879-1700
- **BIHI Women in Action**, 122 W. Franklin Ave., #306, St. Paul, 870-1193. Information, education and referrals for women of color.
- **Centre for Asians and Pacific Islanders**, 3702 E. Lake St. #101, Minneapolis, 721-0122. Employment training, emergency services.
- **Centro Cultural Chicano**, 2025 Nicollet Ave. S., Minneapolis., 874-1412
- **Hmong-American Partnership**, 1525 Glenwood Ave., Minneapolis, 377-6482
- **Jewish Community Center of Greater Minneapolis**, 4330 S. Cedar Lake Rd., St. Louis Park, 377-8330
- **Urban League**: Minneapolis: 407 E. 38th St., 823-5818; St. Paul: 4001 Selby Ave., 224-5771

Disability Assistance

- **Accessible Space**, 2550 University Ave. W., #330N, St. Paul, 645-7271
- **Alliance for the Mentally Ill**, 970 Raymond Ave., St. Paul, 645-2948
- **ARC**, 3225 Lyndale Ave. S., Minneapolis, 827-5641
- **Courage Center**, 3915 Golden Valley Rd., Golden Valley, 588-0811
- **People Incorporated**, 317 York Ave., St. Paul, 774-0011
- **Sister Kenny Institute**, 800 E. 28th St., Minneapolis, 863-4400

Environment

- **Clean Water Action**, 326 Hennepin Ave. E., Minneapolis, 623-3666
- **Greenpeace**, 212 3rd Ave. N., Minneapolis, 333-1917
- **Land Stewardship Project**, 2200 4th St., White Bear Lake, 653-0618
- **Minnesota Center for Environmental Advocacy**, 26 E. Exchange St., St. Paul, 223-5969
- **Minnesota Renewable Energy Society**, Inc., 2928 5th Ave. S., Minneapolis, 781-3585
- **Nature Conservancy**, Minnesota Chapter, 1313 5th St., SE, Minneapolis, 331-0750
- **Sierra Club**, North Star Chapter, 1313 5th St. SE, Minneapolis, 379-3853

Gay and Lesbian

- **Focus Point Newspaper**, 288-9000. Call for a G/L business and organization directory.
- **Gay & Lesbian Community Action Council,** 310 E. 38th St., Minneapolis, 822-0127
- **Parents, Friends and Families of Lesbians and Gays (PFLAG)**, P.O. Box 8588, Minneapolis, 458-3240
- **Pride Institute**, 14400 Martin Dr., Eden Prairie, 934-7554. Chemical dependency counseling.

Health and Hospitals

Most hospitals welcome volunteers—give the nearest one a call. For specific health issues, try the following.

- **Alzheimer's Association**, 8053 E. Bloomington Frwy., Bloomington, 888-7653
- **American Cancer Society**, 3316 W. 66th St., Edina, 925-2772
- **American Heart Association**, 4701 W. 77th St., Edina, 835-3300

- **Planned Parenthood of Minnesota**: St. Paul: 1965 Ford Pkwy., 698-2406, 1700 Rice St., 489-1328; Minneapolis: 1200 Lagoon Ave., 823-6300

Homeless Services

- **Catholic Charities**, 404 S. 8th St., Minneapolis, 340-7500
- **People Serving People**, 917 5th Ave. S., Minneapolis, 333-1221
- **St. Stephen's Shelter**, 2211 Clinton Ave., Minneapolis, 874-9292
- **Salvation Army**, 2300 Freeway Blvd., Brooklyn Center, 566-2040; P.O. Box 75366, St. Paul, 730-6160

Human Services

- **American Red Cross**: Minneapolis: 871-7676; St. Paul: 291-6789
- **Amicus**, 100 N. 6th St. #347B, Minneapolis, 348-8570. Human services for ex-inmates.
- **Citizens' Council**, Minneapolis, 340-5432. Assistance to families of inmates, victims; mediation.
- **Neighborhood Involvement Program**, 2431 Hennepin Ave. S., Minneapolis, 374-3125
- **Phyllis Wheatley Community Center**, 919 Fremont Ave. N., Minneapolis, 374-4342
- **Second Harvest Food Bank**, 484-5117
- **Sharing and Caring Hands**, 425 N. 7th St., Minneapolis, 338-4640

Legal Aid

- **American Civil Liberties Union**, 1021 W. Broadway, Minneapolis, 522-2423
- **Legal Aid Society**, 334-5970
- **Legal Rights Center**, 808 E. Franklin Ave., Minneapolis, 337-0030

Literacy

- **English Learning Center for Immigrants and Refugee Families**, 2315 Chicago Ave. S., Minneapolis, 827-4709
- **Minnesota Literacy Council**, 475 N. Cleveland Ave. #303, St. Paul, 645-2277

Men's Services

- **Domestic Rights Coalition**, 774-7010
- **The Fathers Resource Center**, 430 Oak Grove St. #105, Minneapolis, 874-1509

Politics–Electoral

- **Democratic-Farmer-Labor Party** (Democrats), State Office, 293-1200
- **Independent Republican Party** (Republicans), State Office, 222-0022
- **League of Women Voters of Minnesota**, 550 Rice St., St. Paul, 224-5445

Politics–Social

- **Association of Community Organizations for Reform Now (ACORN)**, 757 Raymond Ave., #200, St. Paul, 642-9639
- **Common Cause in Minnesota**, 1010 University Ave. W., St. Paul, 644-1844
- **Friends for a Nonviolent World**, 1929 S. 5th St., Minneapolis, 321-9787
- **Minnesota Public Interest Research Group (MPIRG)**, 2414 University Ave. SE, Minneapolis, 627-4035

Refugee Assistance

- **American Refugee Committee**, 2344 Nicollet Ave. S., #350, Minneapolis, 872-7060. Health services for foreign refugees.

Senior Services

- **Area Agency on Aging**, 1600 University Ave. W., St. Paul, 641-8612
- **Gray Panthers of the Twin Cities**, 3255 Hennepin Ave. S., Minneapolis, 822-1011
- **Senior Resources**, 331-4063

Women's Services

- **Domestic Abuse Project**, 204 W. Franklin Ave., Minneapolis, 874-7063
- **Minnesota Women's Press**, 771 Raymond Ave., St. Paul, 646-3968. Call for a directory of women's businesses and organizations.
- **Sexual Offense Services of Ramsey County**, 1619 Dayton Ave., #201, St. Paul, 298-5898
- **Sexual Violence Center of Hennepin County**, 2100 Pillsbury Ave. S., Minneapolis, 871-5100
- **Women's Consortium of Minnesota**, 550 Rice St. #101, St. Paul, 228-0338

- **Women of Color Health Alternatives Network**, 1060 Central Ave. W., St. Paul, 646-3775

Youth

- **The Bridge for Runaway Youth**, 2200 Emerson Ave. S., Minneapolis, 377-8800
- **Inner City Youth League**, 905 Selby Ave., St. Paul, 221-9827
- **Project Offstreets**, 212 2nd Ave. N., Minneapolis, 338-3103

Whether recreation to you means breaking a sweat, or cracking a beverage while someone else sweats (or both), year around there's plenty for you in Minneapolis and St. Paul. To the hale and hearty, the climate changes here are just opportunities for more kinds of recreation. And, although the area doesn't offer everything—in a crushing move, the North Stars National Hockey League team moved to Dallas—you're guaranteed to find many invigorating experiences. Have fun, and drink enough liquids.

Spectator Sports

Professional Baseball

Not only do the Twin Cities have a major league baseball team; they're also home to a minor league team that has a loyal following and offers great entertainment value. And there's another minor league team in Austin, a short road trip to the south.

The American League **Minnesota Twins** play 80 or so games a year in the Metrodome, however, they're lobbying for subsidies to build an uncovered stadium, so they may move. For tickets, call 33-TWINS. You can also get Twins tickets from electronic kiosks at Rainbow Foods and other stores.

The **St. Paul Saints** play in the Northern League (A). They play dozens of home games at the tiny outdoor Municipal Stadium in St. Paul's Midway. Off-diamond features include grandstand massages, a pig mascot that carries out the ball, and more. Call **644-6659** for ticket information.

The **Austin Southern Mini-Stars**, an AA team, play at Markesan Park in the hometown of Hormel Foods, makers of Spam. It's about an hour-and-a-half's drive south of the Twin Cities—make it the end destination of a day trip. For tickets, call **507-437-2621**.

Professional Basketball

The NBA's **Minnesota Timberwolves** recently went through the scare of a possible move out of state, but they appear to be here to stay after a local millionaire and the state chipped in to buy their home base, the Target Center, which is in downtown Minneapolis. For game tickets, call Ticketmaster at **989-5151**.

Professional Football

The **Minnesota Vikings** are perennial contenders in the National Football League. They play eight home season games at the Metrodome, as well as pre-season games. The NFL schedule comes out in May. Get tickets early, there aren't many games, and they often sell out. For tickets, call **333-8828**.

Professional Soccer

The fast action and grace of soccer can be enjoyed by watching the **Minnesota Thunder** at the National Sports Center in the northern suburb of Blaine. Call **785-3668** for tickets.

College Sports

College sports, while not as smooth as the pros, are a lot of fun—something about the youthful energy of the players and the crowds—and there's plenty of that to be had here. Call a local college for season and schedule information (see "Colleges and Universities" section in the "Cultural Life" chapter for telephone numbers). The biggest college sports draw here is, of course, the University of Minnesota, which plays in the Big Ten Conference.

> **Baseball** - The University of Minnesota Golden Gophers men's baseball team plays at Siebert Field. The women's softball team games plays at Bierman Field. Call **624-8080** for more information.

> **Basketball** - College basketball has quite a following here, especially the women's team. The Women's Final Four tournament was held in Minneapolis recently, and it may return. University of Minnesota's Golden Gopher men play at Williams Arena, and the women play at the Sports Pavilion. For tickets call **624-8080**.

> **Football** - The University of Minnesota Golden Gophers play in the Big Ten Conference of the Midwest. Home games are held at the Metrodome, so you don't have to worry about hypothermia. For season information and schedules, call **624-8080**.

Hockey - The popular U of M Golden Gophers have always been a power in their conference. They play at Mariucci Arena. Call **624-8080** for ticket information.

Other Spectator Sports

Twin Cities Marathon - First held in 1982, this 26 mile road race begins at the Metrodome in Minneapolis, winds along the Mississippi gorge, and finishes at the St. Paul Cathedral. It's an entertaining event held in the crisp beauty of October that attracts thousands of runners and many more fans. Call **673-0778**.

American Birkebeiner - Hayward, Wisconsin, about three hours' drive from the Twin Cities, is the site of this world-famous 50 kilometer cross-country ski race held each February. The "Birkie," as it's affectionately known, starts at the Telemark ski resort. Thousands come out to see the frosty faces and lycra tights, and to do some skiing themselves. Call 715-634-3345.

Participant Sports-Teams

The parks are alive in the summer with the thud of bat against softball, but that's not the only sport you can join a team to play. Your workplace may sponsor intramural teams for several sports, including the local winter favorite: broomball (a hockey-like game that's played on ice wearing boots not skates and using a volleyball-sized ball rather than a puck and brooms instead of sticks). Otherwise, call the following intramural sports organizing entities:

- **Minnesota Recreation and Park Association**, 5005 W. 36th St., St. Louis Park, 920-6906. Organizes state tournaments for volleyball, basketball, broomball, and touch football.

- **University of Minnesota Sports Clubs**, 900 University Ave. SE, 306 Cooke Hall, Minneapolis, 625-6017. Dozens upon dozens of clubs, primarily for students, but not exclusively so.

Individual Sports

Bicycling

People here bike a *lot*. Minnesota leads the nation in the number of bikes per capita. Bike commuting has tripled from 1970 to 1990 in Minneapolis. It's not unusual to see bikers wheeling to and from work, with any degree of formal attire, particularly in and near both downtowns. Minneapolis accommodates bike commuters as much as possible. Six off-street bike routes are either built or are under construction, many of them on old railroad beds. The city is also collaborating with other metro-area municipalities on a $30 million five-year development plan, which will link existing trails and lanes in a wide web going from the western suburbs all the way to Stillwater. Many of those paths are already built.

In and around the cities, try these routes:

The lakes and greenbelt in Minneapolis. You can travel separately from cars much of the way. Stinson Boulevard, the link between parkways on the northeast side and the West Bank, is supposed to get a commuter path which will complete a magnificent circle of about 25 miles of bike paths around the city.

The 29th Street "Midtown Greenway" in Minneapolis. Projected to be finished by the end of 1996, this route follows a railroad bed one block north of Lake Street from Lake Calhoun to the Mississippi.

The Mississippi River, from Fort Snelling State Park to the U of M campus, on both sides of the river. It's a good bird watching route. On the St. Paul side, take the river parkway all the way south to the Crosby Farm Nature Area.

Summit Avenue, from the Mississippi River to the St. Paul Cathedral, offers a separate bike lane of about five miles.

The Gateway Trail. It begins just south of Wheelock Parkway and east of I-35E in St. Paul, and extends 17 miles to Stillwater, on the Wisconsin border.

Gunflint Trail. For the more ambitious, a 68-mile trip (one-way) that begins in Grand Marais on Lake Superior, winds through hardwoods and pine forests, and ends up in the heart of the Boundary Waters.

For more maps to more routes (there are many more) call the following numbers:

- **Minneapolis Parks and Recreation Board**, 661-4875
- **St. Paul Division of Parks and Recreation**, 266-6400
- **Hennepin County Parks**, 559-9000
- **Ramsey County Parks**, 777-1707
- **Washington County Park Division**, 731-3851
- **Minnesota Department of Natural Resources**, 296-6157

To rent some wheels, visit the following places (also, see the chapter **Shopping for the Home** in this book).

- **The Alternative Bike Shop**, 2408 Hennepin Ave. S., Minneapolis, 374-3635
- **Now Sports Cycling and Fitness**, 75 N. Snelling Ave., St. Paul, 644-2354

Boating

It's not called the Land of Ten Thousand Lakes for nothing. There are hundreds of lakes within the metro area alone, and most of them are used by boats of some kind. Many of them are connected by rivers, marshes and estuaries, all of which offer splendid paddling and communing with nature. If you've got a craft, you'll need a license and some suggestions on where to put in. A **boat license** is good for two years, and its cost depends on your type of boat. For a license application, call the **DNR License Bureau**, 500 Lafayette Rd., St. Paul, **296-2316**. For boating and canoe route suggestions, call the DNR at **296-6157**.

There is a public motorboat marina in St. Paul, on the Mississippi. From it you can tool around the Mississippi, Minnesota and St. Croix Rivers. Call the **Watergate Marina**, 2500 Crosby Farm Rd., St. Paul, **292-7526**.

If a more remote experience is what you're looking for, the **Boundary Waters National Canoe Area-Quetico Provincial Park** should be considered. It's a magnificent expanse of granite outcroppings, lakes and rivers connected by portage trails. Motorboat access is limited (completely banned on the Quetico side, in Canada). Often, the only noises to be heard are the laughing of the loons. Also, there's **Voyageurs National Park**, a stretch of pine forests and water on the Canadian border that's home to the nation's largest wild wolf population. You need to call early in the spring to reserve summer time in these parks. Boundary Waters information is **218-365-7681**. For information on Voyageurs National Park, call **218-283-9821**.

If you're looking for a boat to use nearby, call one of the following **boat rental services**. Most of the popular lakes Up North have plenty of rentals on location.

- **Blue Waters Sailing School**, 2337 Medicine Lake Dr. W,, Plymouth, 559-5649. Sailboats only.
- **Como Lakeside**, 1360 N. Lexington Pkwy., St. Paul, 488-4927. Canoes and paddleboats.
- **Minneapolis Parks:** The park system rents canoes and paddleboats at many of the metro area lakes. Call 661-4875 for rental information on Minneapolis lakes; call 559-9000 for metro-area lakes outside the city.
- **Midwest Mountaineering**, 309 Cedar Ave. S., Minneapolis, 339-3433. Canoes, kayaks.

Bowling

You betcha! Bowling is an integral part of local culture. It's a sport of concentration, but it's also a casual night out. There's even a bowling alley with a wine and espresso bar and performance space—the Bryant-Lake Bowl—listed below with a selection of other lanes.

- **Bryant-Lake Bowl**, 810 W. Lake St., Minneapolis, 825-3737
- **Fairlanes Apache Plaza**, 3800 Silver Lake Rd., St. Anthony, 788-9128
- **Maplewood Bowl**, 1955 English St., Maplewood, 774-8787
- **Midway Pro Bowl**, 1556 University Ave., St. Paul, 646-1396
- **Nokomis Lanes**, 4040 Bloomington Ave. S., Minneapolis, 827-1781
- **West Side Lanes**, 1625 S. Robert St., West St. Paul, 451-6222

Curling

If you've always wanted to bowl outdoors in the winter, the closest you'll come to fulfilling your dream is this old-fashioned game of hand-eye coordination that uses "curling stones" and is played on ice that you must polish. Contact the **St. Paul Curling Club**, 470 Selby Ave., St. Paul, **224-7408**.

Fishing

The Minnesota fishing license can seem as prevalent as the Minnesota drivers' license. Fishing season opener in the spring creates a big splash in the media, as thousands of anglers flock to the prize lakes Up North. Typically, a cottage is the destination, so the expression goes, "I was gone fishing at the cottage up north." The Department of Natural Resources stocks lakes in the metro area as well as those Up North. Don't forget ice fishing, either. For information on a **fishing license**, call **296-4506**. Regulations are Byzantine in complexity. For a brochure on catch rules and information about the best lakes, call the **Fishing Division of the DNR**, at **296-3325**.

Golf

Having just moved, you may not be quite ready to join a country club. But you do want to play a round . . . not to worry; there are plenty of fine municipal golf courses in the metro area. Choose from these courses, or call the **Minnesota Golf Association**, at **927-4643**.

- **Braemer Golf Course**, 6364 John Harris Dr., Edina, 941-2072
- **Brookview Golf Course**, 200 Brookview Pkwy., Golden Valley, 544-8446
- **Columbia Golf Course**, 3300 Central Ave. NE, Minneapolis, 789-2627
- **Como Park Golf Course**, 1431 N. Lexington Pkwy., St. Paul, 488-9673
- **Francis A. Gross Golf Course**, 2201 St. Anthony Blvd., St. Anthony, 789-2542
- **Highland Park Golf Course**, 1403 Montreal Ave., St. Paul, 699-0193

- **Hiawatha Golf Course**, 4553 Longfellow Ave., Minneapolis, 724-7715
- **Keller Golf Course**, 2166 Maplewood Dr., Maplewood, 484-3011
- **Phalen Park Golf Course**, 1615 Phalen Dr., 778-0424
- **Theodore Wirth Golf Course**, 1301 Wirth Pkwy. N., Minneapolis, 522-4584

Health Clubs & Gyms/YMCAs & YWCAs

If you work for a larger company, ask human resources about any company discounts being offered by fitness centers. Or, try these:

- **Arena Health Club**, 600 1st Ave. N., Minneapolis, 673-1200
- **Bally Total Fitness**. For the nearest location, call 1-800-695-8111
- **Calhoun Beach Club Inc.**, 2925 Dean Pkwy., Minneapolis, 927-9951
- **Lilydale Club**, 945 Sibley Memorial Hwy., Lilydale, 457-4954
- **Northwest Racquet, Swim & Health Clubs**, 5525 Cedar Lake Road, St. Louis Park, for many other locations, call 525-2582 or 546-5474
- **Regency Athletic Club and Spa**, 1300 Nicollet Ave., Minneapolis, 343-3131
- **St. Clair Racquet Club**, 1560 St. Clair Ave., St. Paul, 690-0600
- **The University Club**, 420 Summit Ave., St. Paul, 222-1751

If you're attending a college or university, inquire about gym privileges that probably come as part of your enrollment. If you're on a budget but want to exercise year-round, call the following, for a start:

YMCA. A monthly membership costs $39 for one or $63 for a family, with an initiation of fee of $49 in both cases. Volunteering for the Y can get you a discount. Call for locations of numerous branches.

- **Minneapolis**, 30 S. 9th St., 371-8700 (Downtown Branch and Administration)
- **St. Paul**, 476 N. Robert St., 292-4100 (Downtown Branch and Administration)

YWCA. Membership is $45 a month per person (male or female); yearly, it's $588. Call the numbers below for other locations.

- **Minneapolis** (Downtown Branch), 1130 Nicollet Mall, 332-0501; Uptown Branch, 2808 Hennepin Ave. S., 874-7131
- **St. Paul** (administration), 198 N. Western Ave., 222-3741; Fitness Center (same address), 225-9922

Hiking

The amount of green you see on the Minnesota state map speaks for itself—a good part of the northern third of the state is either state or national forest. There are dozens of state parks nearby and four national parks within a day's drive.

For information on some interesting hikes to take right around town, talk to the **Minneapolis Municipal Hiking Club**, at **661-4875**. Following are some suggestions for wilderness hikes. For complete listings and descriptions of the state's parks, call the **DNR's Parks and Recreation Division**, at **296-6157**. The annual state park pass is a bargain at $18. Camping costs a few extra dollars per night beyond an entrance fee; make reservations at **800-246-2267** (locally 922-9000). Note: mid-September to mid-October is the peak time for fall colors. The local media report on the progress of color changes with maps and elaborate descriptions. There's no denying it's a picturesque time for hiking, but the price may be city-size traffic jams—just a warning.

Hiking Nearby:

- **Afton State Park**, Hastings, 436-5391. Hike the rolling bluffs along the St. Croix River.
- **Fort Snelling State Park**, Hwys. 5 & 55, St. Paul, 725-2390. Historic site; trails that connect to the metro parkways.
- **Hyland Lake Park Reserve**, Hwy. 28, Bloomington, 941-4362. Nice meadow trails.
- **St. Croix River State Park**, Hinckley, 612-384-6591. Lush bluffside hiking, joins up with other parks along the St. Croix.
- **North Hennepin Trail Corridor**, 424-5511 or 424-8172. Paved trails connecting two park preserves in the western suburbs.

Hiking A Day's Drive Away:

- **Badlands National Park**, Rapid City, South Dakota, 605-433-5362. Forgive the disloyalty to Minnesota, but this national treasure can be reached by nightfall if you leave early. For other hiking ideas in the area, call the Black Hills National Forest Ranger, at 605-673-4853.
- **Isle Royale National Park**, Houghton, Michigan, 906-482-0984. A half-day's drive to Grand Portage, and you can take the 22-mile ferry ride across Lake Superior the next morning. Mingle with wolves, moose, wildflowers and the Windigo spirit on this remote island. There's also a lodge with full amenities, for post-hike luxury.
- **North Country National Scenic Trail**, Walker, near Leech Lake. A 68-mile backpacking trail in the rolling hills and hardwood forests of northern Minnesota. It's part of a national plan that will join it with the Appalachian Trail in New York and the Lewis and Clark Trail in North Dakota. For information call the Chippewa National Forest at 218-335-8600.

- **Superior National Forest**, northeast corner of state. For camping and hiking information call 218-720-5324. Hundreds of miles of hiking trails are marked out in parks within this area. The North Shore State Trail is a 70-mile route from Duluth to Grand Marais. The trailhead is in Finland, off State Route 1.

Horseback Riding

Ask about sleigh rides and carriage rides as well.

- **Anderson Livery**, 658 Bolton Ave. SW, Buffalo, 682-2521. Open year 'round.
- **Brass Ring Stables**, 9105 Norris Lake Rd., Elk River, 441-7987
- **City Lights Carriage**, 995 Bayless Ave., St. Paul, 860-1799. Make reservations here for city carriage rides.
- **Diamond T Riding Stable**, 4889 Pilot Knob Rd., Eagan, 454-1464

Ice Skating

If you enjoy gliding across a smooth lake surface under the stars, you've come to the right neck of the woods. Nearly every lake in the Twin Cities has a rink and warming house in the winter, and they're lighted at night. If you're not a skater (yet), just watching a slow circle of skaters can be meditative. Hockey leagues play and practice on separate rinks. The following are covered rinks, which offer some protection from the elements.

- **Adams Arena**, 743 Western Ave. N., St. Paul, 488-1336
- **Braemer Arena**, 7501 Hwy. 169, Edina, 941-1322. Open year-round.
- **Breck School Ice Arena**, 5800 Wayzata Blvd., Minneapolis, 545-1614
- **Highland Arena**, 800 Snelling Ave. S., St. Paul, 699-7156
- **Hopkins Pavilion**, 1515 Cty. Rd. 3, Hopkins, 939-1410
- **Minnehaha Academy**, 4200 W. River Pkwy., Minneapolis, 729-8770
- **Phalen Arena**, 1320 Walsh St., St. Paul, 776-2554
- **Roseville Ice Arena**, 2661 Civic Center Dr., Roseville, 484-0268. Year 'round.
- **Victory Memorial Ice Arena**, 1900 42nd Ave. N., Minneapolis, 627-2952. Open year 'round.
- **Yackel West Side Arena**, 44 E. Isabel, St. Paul, 228-1145

You may rent skates from the following places, among others.

- **Pierce Skate and Ski**, 208 W. 98th St., Bloomington, 884-1990
- **Penn Cycle**, 710 W. Lake St., Minneapolis, 822-2228
- **Macalester Bicycle and Ski Exchange**, 370 S. Snelling Ave., St. Paul, 698-3966

For beginning ice-skating instruction, a good resource is the park centers themselves (listed below). For more formal training, call the schools listed below.

- **Minneapolis Parks and Recreation Board**, 661-4875
- **St. Paul Division of Parks and Recreation**, 266-6400
- **Breck School Ice Arena**, 5800 Wayzata Blvd., Minneapolis, 545-1614
- **Minnehaha Academy**, 4200 W. River Pkwy., Minneapolis, 729-8770

In-line Skating

It is fitting that in the home of the Rollerblade®, one of the most popular warm-weather activities is to strap on in-line skates and cruise the marvelous lake and greenbelt path system. Heavily used lake routes, such as along Lake Calhoun and Lake of the Isles, have separate paths for people on and off wheels, so in-line skaters can mix it up with bikers. The Summit Avenue bike lane and Mississippi River parkways are righteous in-line routes as well. In the winter, the hallways of the **Metrodome** (825-3663) are regularly opened to in-line skaters. It's spacious, and it's the home of the Vikings. What more could you ask for? Or try the following, among many others:

- **Roller Garden**, 5622 W. Lake St., St. Louis Park, 929-5518. Lessons available.
- **Roseville Ice Arena**, 2661 Civic Center Dr., Roseville, 484-0268

For rentals, try these places for starters:

- **Penn Cycle**, 710 W. Lake St., Minneapolis, 822-2228
- **Macalester Bicycle and Ski Exchange**, 370 S. Snelling Ave., St. Paul, 698-3966
- **Rolling Soles**, 1700 W. Lake St., Minneapolis, 823-5711

Racquet Sports

The courts listed here are either public courts or private institutions that offer daily rates for non-members. Keep in mind that many health clubs contain indoor tennis courts; see listings. All of the following are indoor courts except for the Minikahda Club, which is worth mentioning because of its high quality clay courts (usable from April through October). Other outdoor courts can be found at parks and school yards throughout town. For other racquet sports, see the health clubs listing. For more information, call the Northwestern Tennis Association, 5525 Cedar Lake Rd., St. Louis Park, 546-0709.

- **Daytona Club**, 14740 N. Lawndale Ln., Dayton, 427-6110
- **Minikahda Club**, 3520 Xenith Ave. S., Minneapolis, 924-1663
- **Northwest Racquet, Swim & Health Clubs**, 5525 Cedar Lake Road, St. Louis Park, for many other locations, call 525-2582 or 546-5474
- **Nicollet Tennis Center**, 4005 Nicollet Ave., Minneapolis, 825-6844
- **Regency Athletic Club and Spa**, 1300 Nicollet Mall, Minneapolis, 343-3131
- **St. Paul Indoor Tennis Club**, 600 DeSoto St., St. Paul, 774-2121

Rock Climbing

Okay, so there are no sheer cliff walls at ten thousand feet here. Even so, the granite bluffs of the Upper Midwest, where they haven't been worked over by glaciers, do offer some worthy challenges to climbers.

The best rock climbs nearby are the quartzite bluffs at **Devil's Lake State Park** near Baraboo, Wisconsin, about a four hour drive Southeast. It's a beautiful hiking area, too. Call **608-356-8301**. Climbers also like the sheer basalt walls on the banks of the St. Croix River at **Interstate State Park in Taylors Falls**. The number there is **612-465-5711**. To practice on indoor walls, visit the following places:

- **Footprints Adventure**, 9208 James Ave. S., Bloomington, 884-7996
- **Midwest Mountaineering**, 309 Cedar Ave. S., Minneapolis, 339-3433
- **Vertical Endeavors**, 844 Arcade St., St. Paul, 776-1430

Running

Even in the dead of January you can see many hardy Minnesotans jogging along the streets and parkways. The parkway system around the lakes is popular with runners, as is the system of paths on both sides of the Mississippi from Fort Snelling to the U of M. For route suggestions, race information and running mates, call the following numbers. Also listed is an annual event that (briefly) transforms distance running here into a spectator sport, the Twin Cities Marathon (more about this race can be found in the "Spectator Sports" section of this chapter).

- **Minnesota Distance Running Association**, 5701 Normandale Rd., Edina, 927-0983. Race Hotline: 925-4749.
- **Team Run N Fun**, 868 Randolph Ave., St. Paul, 290-2747. Informal running group, meets twice a month.
- **Hash House Harriers of the Twin Cities**. Non-competitive irreverent runs, unusual routes, according to an old British game. Information line, 452-2708.
- **Twin Cities Marathon**. Held in October. Call 673-0778.

Scuba Diving

If you dive around here, you're more likely to see muskellunges than manta rays but that can be thrilling too. Good dives nearby are found at Square Lake County Park in Washington County and Devil's Lake near Baraboo, Wisconsin. The following places can get you certified and equipped.

- **Scuba Dive and Travel**, 4741 Chicago Ave. S., Minneapolis, 823-7210
- **Scuba Daddy's Dive Shop**, 14844 Granada Ave., Apple Valley, 432-7070

Skiing–Cross Country

Once it snows, cross country ski tracks magically appear at all of the larger parks and golf courses in the cities. You can follow them or if you want to get out into the woods and forge your own twin tracks, try just about any of the State Parks listed in the "Hiking" section of this chapter. You must purchase a $5 cross country ski pass in addition to the park sticker. The state **DNR** issues trail passes; call **296-4506**. Ski stores sell them, too.

For an invigorating winter getaway, rent a cabin on the **North Shore** (the arrowhead-shaped part of the state north of Duluth), and tour the area's granite bluffs and woods by cross-country skis. To get a package of North Shore tourist information, call **218-722-4011**. Also, the **Boundary Waters Canoe Area** is open to cross country skiers in the winter (a more isolated experience). Call **218-365-7681**. Nearby in Wisconsin, **Telemark Lodge** has miles of well-groomed cross-country ski trails and hosts the world-famous Birkebeiner ski race. Call **715-798-3811**. For statewide snow conditions, call the **DNR's 24-hour snow hotline** at **296-6157** or **800-657-3700**.

Both park districts offer free cross country ski lessons. Call the following numbers for more information:

- **Minneapolis Parks and Recreation Board**   661-4875
- **St. Paul Division of Parks and Recreation**   266-6400

For rental, sales, and advice, try the following (among others):

- **Aarcee Recreation**, 2910 Lyndale Ave. S., Minneapolis, 827-5746
- **Joe's Ski Shop**, 935 N. Dale St., St. Paul, 488-5511
- **Midwest Mountaineering**, 309 Cedar Ave. S., Minneapolis, 339-3433
- **North Country Inc.**, 8980 E. Hudson Blvd., St. Paul, 739-3500

Skiing—Downhill

The definitive downhill skiing experience is only a full day's drive to the southwest, in Colorado. Slopes closer by, however, offer a fun day out, and snowboarding and snow skating are available at some of them as well. Try the following areas, most of which have rentals available at the lodge. For snow information call the DNR's Snow Hotline at 296-6167 or 800-657-3700.

- **Afton Alps**, 6600 Peller Ave. S., Afton, 436-5245
- **Andes Tower Hills**, 4505 Andes Rd. SW, Kensington, 612-965-2455
- **Hyland Hills Ski Area and School**, 8800 Chalet Rd., Bloomington, 835-4604
- **Indianhead Mountain**, Wakefield, Michigan, 800-3INDIAN
- **Lutsen Mountain Ski Area**, Lutsen, 218-663-7281
- **Rib Mountain**, Wausau, Wisconsin, 715-845-2846
- **Spirit Mountain**, Duluth, 800-642-6377
- **Wild Mountain Ski Area**, Taylors Falls, 800-447-4958

Snowmobiling

In winter, this is the state "sport" for Minnesotans who love their motorized vehicles. The first business listed has snowmobiles for rent; the second offers destination ideas. Also call the DNR general information number (296-6157) for locations of trails.

- **Bay Rentals Inc.**, Minnetonka, 474-0366, mobile phone: 750-5262
- **Snowmobile Vacation Guide**, 601 Lakeshore Pkwy., Minnetonka, 476-2200 (published in the December issue of Snowgoer magazine)

Swimming Beaches

Beaches in the metro area are guarded from early June to mid-August. None are open to dogs. For more information, call either Minneapolis Parks, at 661-4875; Hennepin County Parks (for beaches outside the city) at 559-9000, or Ramsey County Parks, at 777-1707.

Minneapolis Beaches

- **Cedar Lake**, South Shore on Cedar Lake Pkwy.; First St. at Cedar Lake Pkwy.
- **Lake Calhoun**, North Shore at Lake St.; 32nd St. at Calhoun Pkwy.; Thomas Ave. at Calhoun Pkwy.
- **Lake Harriet**, North Shore at Lake Harriet Pkwy.; Minnehaha Pkwy. at Lake Harriet Pkwy.

- **Lake Hiawatha**, 45th St. at 28th Ave. S.
- **Lake Nokomis**, 50th St. at Nokomis Pkwy.; West Shore at 50th St.
- **Wirth Lake**, Glenwood Ave. at Wirth Pkwy.

St. Paul Beaches

- **Lake Como**, Como Blvd. at Horton Ave.
- **Lake Phalen**, Phalen Park on Wheelock Pkwy.

Hennepin County Public Beaches

- **Baker Park Reserve,** County Rds. 19 and 24, Maple Plain
- **Bryant Lake Regional Park**, 6400 Rowland Rd., Eden Prairie
- **Cleary Lake Regional Park**, 18106 Texas Ave. S., Prior Lake
- **Elm Creek Park Preserve**, 13080 Territorial Rd., Maple Grove
- **Fish Lake Regional Park**, 14900 Bass Lake Rd., Maple Grove
- **French Lake Regional Park**, 12615 Cty. Rd. 9, Plymouth
- **Lake Rebecca Park Preserve**, 9831 Cty. Rd. 50, Rockford

Ramsey County Public Beaches

- **Bald Eagle Lake**, 5800 Hugo Rd., White Bear Township
- **Gervais Lake**, 2520 Edgerton St., Little Canada
- **Lake Johanna,** 3500 Lake Johanna Blvd., Arden Hills
- **Long Lake**, 1500 Old Hwy. 8, New Brighton
- **White Bear Lake**, 5050 Lake Ave., White Bear Lake

Swimming Pools

Minneapolis outdoor swimming pools are open from June to August; in St. Paul, they're open June to September. For additional information on municipal pools, call the same numbers listed (above) for beaches. Once it gets cold, check the YMCA and listings in the "Health Clubs" section of the Yellow Pages.

- **Como Pool**, Como Ave. at Lexington Pkwy. N., St. Paul, 489-2811
- **Highland Pool**, Montreal Ave. at Hamline Ave., St. Paul, 699-7968
- **North Commons**, 1701 Golden Valley Rd. N., Minneapolis, 370-4945
- **Oxford Pool**, Lexington Pkwy. at Iglehart Ave., St. Paul, 647-9925
- **Richfield Municipal Swimming Pool**, 630 E. 66th St., Richfield, 861-9355
- **Rosacker Pool**, 1500 Johnson St. NE, Minneapolis, 370-4937
- **Valley View Pool**, 201 E. 90th St., Bloomington, 881-0900
- **Webber Pool**, 4300 Webber Pkwy. N., Minneapolis, 370-4915

When the most recent ice age ended, approximately ten thousand years ago, the receding glaciers left something behind: a landscape filled with lakes. Today the lakes (and parkways) are considered the jewels of the Twin Cities, a place where all residents, as well as herons and flocks of Canada Geese, can go for recreation and relaxation. Amazingly though, they almost didn't become park land.

By the 1880s, the lakes had become a popular place for resorts, and hotels had begun to encircle Lake Calhoun. State officials wanted to establish the shores of Calhoun, as well as some other prime lakefront areas, as regional parks. They proposed to set up an independent park board to run these areas, hoping that would keep the land away from city hall corruption. Response to the plan was decidedly unenthusiastic. City leaders didn't like giving up direct control over any area of the city; many businessmen thought it was a speculation scheme by conspiratorial insiders; labor leaders agreed (this time) with business. Park proponents prevailed, though, by citing the success of New York's Central Park and promising that the land would remain public. Ten years later, Theodore Wirth marshaled the park system into much of what it is today by adding lands and writing guidelines for the future. Wirth Park is named after him.

The idea was to link the lakes and green spaces together into a coherent system of paths, which are today called the parkways. These parkways serve a variety of uses, including recreation and solitude, and although it's not quite a complete circle, the circuit of Minneapolis greenspace that Wirth originated is today affectionately known as the **Grand Round**. Following is a brief tour of this 30-mile greenbelt as well as other metro-area parks and forests:

Begin at **Minnehaha Park**, a picnic and nature area surrounding a small gorge that empties into the Mississippi. From the northern end of the park, pick up Minnehaha Parkway, heading westward. In about a mile, you'll reach **Lake Nokomis** (picnic grounds, swimming, playing fields). **Hiawatha Golf Course**, with Lake Hiawatha, is adjacent to the north. You can do a loop of about 3 miles around Lake Nokomis or continue on. Approximately 5 miles further, you'll come upon **Lake Harriet**.

The park here offers picnic spots, beaches, and the lovely **Lake Harriet Rock Garden**, with dwarf conifers, flowering trees and perennials, as well as the **Lake Harriet Pavilion** which features summer concerts. Travel along Lake Harriet; a full circle around it is close to 3 miles.

From the north end of Lake Harriet it's a short jog to **Lake Calhoun**. The Lake Calhoun parkway is thick with runners, bikers and skaters most of the year. The trip around the lake is about 3-1/2 miles. The shores of Lake Calhoun are host to volleyball games, picnics, paddleboats, sailboats, canoes, and sunbathers (at the right time of the year). Lunch at an Uptown cafe is just a short walk from the eastern shore of the lake.

About two miles east of Lake Calhoun and a couple of blocks south of Lake Street is a park not directly connected to the parkway system but no less used and appreciated, **Powderhorn Park**. The park got its name from the crescent "powderhorn" shape Powderhorn Lake originally had, although the lake lost that look when it was dug out at the turn of the century to drain away wetlands along its shores (wetlands preservation was not yet a concept). Powderhorn Park, a welcome break from the urban surroundings, offers sledding hills, cross-country skiing, and community events.

The parkway continues its circuit of lakes from the northwestern shore of Lake Calhoun to **Cedar Lake**. Another path at the northern tip of Calhoun leads to the oddly-shaped and elegant **Lake of the Isles**. It's a 3-mile trip around. At the northern end of Lake of the Isles you'll notice **Kenwood Park**, a patch of wooded hills with outdoor tennis courts. Returning to Lake Calhoun, the parkway leaves the lake once again and follows one side of Cedar Lake for a mile before heading northward to **Wirth Park**. This park, named for the father of the Minneapolis park system, offers a mix of woods, prairie, picnic areas and beaches. A few marked nature paths wind through the woods.

From Wirth Park, the parkway heads straight north, then cuts due east along a green right-of-way called **Memorial Parkway.** Four miles later, in far-north Minneapolis, it runs into **Shingle Creek Park** and **Webber Park**, which border the banks of the Mississippi. You can cross the river on 42nd Avenue, then pick up St. Anthony Parkway on the other side. Here, you can follow the parkway for three miles across Northeast Minneapolis to Stinson Boulevard. That's where the parkways end, unfortunately. A path down Stinson Boulevard leading to the East Bank of the Mississippi will soon be finished, to complete the magnificent circle of separated paths around the city known as the grand round.

Another place to tour the parkways is along the **Mississippi River**. The parkways along either bank are good bird watching areas. Begin at the Hennepin Avenue bridge in downtown Minneapolis. You can follow West River Parkway and eventually reach **Minnehaha Park** on the city's far south side. Hennepin Avenue bridge crosses over **Nicollet Island Park** to the city's original Main Street on the east bank. From Main Street, you could cross back to the west bank on the **Stone Arch Bridge**, built by James J. Hill 150 years ago and now the exclusive domain of pedestrians and bicyclists. You could also follow East River

Parkway south, going through the University of Minnesota campus, then eventually pass **Hidden Falls Park**, a picnic area on the riverbank. A little further along the parkway is **Fort Snelling State Park**, the site of a stone fort built on the river bluff in the 1820s. Fort Snelling was the first official European settlement in the upper Midwest. The path ends at **Crosby Farm Nature Area**, a secluded preserve of Mississippi River estuaries and marshes.

Not directly connected to these paths but worth noting is the vast acreage of the **Minnesota River National Wildlife Refuge**, which stretches along the Minnesota River south of Fort Snelling State Park. An interpretive center can be found south of State Highway 5 and I-494 on Old Shakopee Road.

Although not connected by a system of paths, St. Paul's lakes also deserve mention. Besides the Como Park Zoo and Conservatory, **Como Park** offers visitors a public swimming pool, golf course, and a couple of miles of paved paths. In the summer you can rent canoes, paddleboats and bikes here and if you come to Como Park in the winter, ski rentals are available. At the turn of the century, the zoo was moved from Harriet Island downtown. The Victorian-era Como Conservatory has sunken gardens, a grotto and pond. **Phalen Park** offers a large lake, a substantial expanse of rolling hills, a golf course, wooded bluffs, and a paved running path. In the summer visitors may rent sailboats; after it snows the park offers cross country ski lessons. **Pig's Eye Lake Park**, 3 miles downstream from downtown St. Paul, is actually a 500-acre backwater of the Mississippi that serves as a valuable refuge for migrating birds such as great blue herons, egrets, and cormorants.

If you take a look at what's available at Twin Cities parks and lakes, you'll probably agree that Theodore Wirth's original multi-use vision has been made a reality. Check the "Sports and Recreation" chapter, under Boating, Hiking, Swimming and Skiing headings for phone numbers of numerous beaches and suggestions for park use. The **Minneapolis Parks and Recreation Board** can provide information on rentals and lessons in swimming, canoeing, sailing, paddleboats, diving, golf, tennis, windsurfing and more. Also, the **Hennepin Parks District** (for outlying areas) can provide particulars on canoe, kayak, mountain bike trips and lessons, as well as wildflower and bird watching hikes. For information on beaches, trails and rentals in **St. Paul** and **Ramsey County Parks**, call the numbers, listed below.

- **Minneapolis Parks and Recreation**, 661-4875
- **Hennepin County Parks**, 559-9000
- **St. Paul Parks and Recreation**, 266-6400
- **Ramsey County Parks**, 777-1707

Once you've settled in, you'll eventually want to get away, even for a weekend. Celebrate moving in by leaving town and heading to one of the following places. In addition to the locations mentioned below, you may want to join the time-honored tradition of heading "Up North." It doesn't matter where you go; there are ten thousand lakes to choose from, remember? One popular locale to head for is Mille Lacs Lake, about two hours' drive north. If you head up that way, don't miss the giant Paul Bunyan in nearby Brainerd. To reserve a campsite at one of the many state parks Up North or elsewhere, call the DNR's reservation line at 800-246-2267. For general travel information call the **Minnesota Office of Tourism**, 121 Seventh Place East, St. Paul, at **296-5029**. In case your getaway involves skiing, call the state's **Snow Hotline** at **296-6157** or **800-657-3700**. Following are some destinations that can be explored in a weekend's time (of course, more time if you have it).

The North Shore - North of Duluth, to the tip of the "Arrowhead" at Grand Portage, the granite bluffs offer spectacular views of Lake Superior, nice hikes, cross-country skiing, antique shop hunting and raptor-watching, depending on the season. Duluth is a little over two hours' drive north. To get a package of North Shore tourist information, call **218-722-4011**.

Trempealeau - About three hours southeast of the Twin Cities on the Wisconsin side of the Mississippi River, this tiny town has a historic hotel with excellent vegetarian cuisine and live music in the summer. The **Trempealeau Hotel** also rents bikes and canoes which you can use to explore nearby Perrot State Park and the Upper Mississippi National Wildlife Refuge. Spot herons, eagles, trains and river barges. Call **608-534-6898** for more information.

Aveda Spa - The healthy indulgence option. In remote Osceola, less than an hour's drive northeast across the border in Wisconsin, this retreat owned by the shampoo people offers backrubs, complete body-care, gourmet cuisine, and lots of quiet time. **715-294-4465**.

Madison - The Wisconsin capital is about four hours' drive southeast. Stop at **Devil's Lake State Park** on the way—it's a beautiful hiking area with quartzite cliffs (**608-356-8301**). In Madison, enjoy University of Wisconsin events, or take in some live music or theater. **American Players Theater**, a Shakespearean repertory group, performs outdoors in Spring Green in the summer (**608-588-7401**). Taliesen, Frank Lloyd Wright's architecture school, is also near Spring Green. And if you haven't had enough Frank Lloyd Wright, the city of Madison is just finishing the Frank Lloyd Wright Convention Center, which is being built according to a design left behind by Wright.

Chicago - This just squeaks in as a "quick" getaway—it's eight hours' drive one way—but if you give yourself four days, you won't feel rushed. Chicago needs no introduction, but as a reminder, you can visit the Art Institute, the Field Museum of Natural History, the Magnificent Mile of shopping on Michigan Avenue, eclectic shops and pubs on Clark Street, Old Town, blues and jazz festivals, and more. Yes, the Cubs still play at Wrigley Field. To get a packet of information, call the **Chicago Office of Tourism** at **312-744-2400**.

These ideas are only a place to start. Many quiet retreats and entertaining getaways are to be found throughout Minnesota. **Stillwater**, on the scenic St. Croix River, is little more thirty minutes drive from the Cities. Antique shops, elegant Victorian bed-and-breakfast inns and a micro-brewery are some of Stillwater's attractions. There are numerous other such small towns. For a complete guide to off-the-beaten-path Minnesota vacations, locate a copy of *Romancing Minnesota,* by Kate Crowley and Michael Link.

By Car

For better or worse, people in the Twin Cities get around by car. Two-thirds of all commuters working in Minneapolis use a car to get to the office, and 85 percent of those drivers drive alone. Traffic continues to intensify despite carpooling initiatives and road expansions. That's not to say that if you're coming from any of the largest cities in the country, you won't find traffic here downright tolerable, but traffic on the main arteries does often come to a grinding halt during rush hours. Be prepared.

The first thing to watch for on Twin Cities I-roads is the on-ramp green light. The on-ramp signals are meant to keep cars flowing smoothly onto the highway. They're bona fide traffic lights, so yes, you're supposed to stop until the light turns green. Another clever idea from the Department of Transportation: the accident alert sign. Most major arteries have hanging message signs on overpasses that give you early warning of an oncoming traffic-stopper. As you head for an exit, be aware of cars coming from the ever-present on-ramp placed right before an exit. These locations have confused many a new arrival. In general, go as slowly as road conditions dictate; weather here can include freezing rain, snow or near biblical-proportion downpours. Always leave plenty of time to get where you're going. For up-to-the-minute road conditions, call the state **Department of Transportation's road condition hotline** at **800-542-0220**.

As you get to know the Cities, you'll find alternatives to the big roads, but until then, here are some of the **main arteries**:

- The big north-south roadway is I-35. This highway splits in Burnsville into I-35W, which heads into Minneapolis, and I-35E, which goes through St. Paul. The two roads run through the northern suburbs before joining again in Lino Lakes. I-35 ends in Duluth. As you near downtown Minneapolis from the south, keep right to stay headed north on I-35W. Keep right on I-35W to get onto I-94 East, which leads to St. Paul. To the left, State Highway 65 ends quickly downtown. There is also an exit here for I-94 West. A congestion-relief tip: if you're heading for the Uptown area from I-35W, consider heading into downtown and taking a street south instead of getting onto I-94—or get in line and wait.

- Lesser north-south routes serving St. Paul are State Highway 3, which connects southeastern suburbs to downtown St. Paul; State Highway 61, which winds along the Mississippi and cuts northwest into St. Paul (a beautiful drive near the river); and State Highway 5, which goes directly from the airport to West 7th Street.

- Lesser north-south routes on the Minneapolis side are State Highway 77, which is a link from Apple Valley to the Mall of America and the airport; State Highway 100, which runs from Bloomington through first-ring suburbs to Brooklyn Center; and US 169, which runs slightly to the west of 100 from Eden Prairie to Maple Grove, then becomes a state highway heading north. Also, State Highway 280 joins I-94 to State Hwy. 36, an east-west route north of St. Paul.

- I-94 is the main east-west thoroughfare. It does not split in two the way I-35 does, but instead cuts directly through downtown St. Paul, then cuts past downtown Minneapolis. I-94 then turns due north before heading out of town to the northwest. To continue eastward, get onto I-394 (which becomes US 12) or state Highway 55.

- Minor east-west arteries are State Highway 62 (the Crosstown), which runs from Minnetonka to the airport, and I-394 and US 12 which head out of downtown Minneapolis together; I-394 ends at State Highway 100, while US 12 keeps continues due west out of the metro area as a state highway. The other east-west route is State Highway 36, which runs through suburbs north of St. Paul to Stillwater.

- The main encircling arteries are I-694 to the north and I-494 to the south and west. Minneapolis - St. Paul International Airport is on I-94 in Bloomington; see below for best routes by which to approach it. The Mall of America is on I-494 in Bloomington.

Once you've been on these routes enough times, you may look for alternatives through the city streets. Also consider carpooling. **Minnesota Rideshare** links people who want rides with others who work in the same area. Call them at **349-RIDE**.

By Bus

Unfortunately, the only mass transit now available is the bus system. Boosters of a light rail system are ever hopeful, but prospects for it remain dim. The well-run bus system, called **Metropolitan Council Transit Operations (MCTO)**, has tried to keep up with the pace of sprawl in the metro area. You can travel by bus along many of the larger streets, into and between the two downtowns, and from the downtowns to many suburban areas. If you live in outlying areas, you can park at a designated lot and bus into town. Bus stops are marked with the "T" logo.

The first thing you should do is know this number: **373-3333**. You can call it to have a transit system map mailed to you, to find out about routes and schedules, to contact the lost and found service, or for almost anything else related to municipal bus service. If you want to pick up a map, talk to someone in person, and buy a pass all in the same trip, visit one of the following MCTO Transit Stores (or reach them by calling the above number):

- Minneapolis Transit Store, 719 Marquette Ave., open 7:30 a.m. to 5:30 P.M. weekdays
- St. Paul Transit Store, Fifth St. at Minnesota St. in the American National Bank building, open 7:30 a.m. to 5 p.m. weekdays
- Mall of America Transit Store, 60 E. Broadway (in the transit station), open 11:30 a.m. to 7 p.m. Tuesday through Saturday

A base fare ($1.50) gets you one ride plus two transfers to complete a trip. Express routes, which travel between the downtowns and to suburbs, cost 50 cents extra. Rush hour fare is also an added 50 cents. You can pay as you go (the driver takes bills, but doesn't make change), buy 10-ride discount passes, or go all-out for a monthly unlimited pass.

If your trip doesn't have a convenient connection, there's one more option. Check the routes and schedules of the **University of Minnesota Transit Service (625-9000)**. U of M buses run from many locations throughout the city to the University. Anyone can ride them, and they cost the same as a city bus.

Outside the Cities, you have four commuting options that don't require your own vehicle. First, you can sign up for a carpool with **Minnesota Rideshare**, which is run by MCTO **(349-RIDE)**. Second, you can get a ride, bike, walk, ski, skate...to a Park N' Ride lot (they're sprinkled throughout the metro area) and catch a bus into town. Call Minnesota Rideshare for information on locations. Third, you can catch a suburban bus line that can probably connect you to a city bus. Call one of the following for schedules:

South

• **Bloomington-Edina Public Transit**	373-3333
• **Minnesota Valley Transit**	882-7500
• **Southwest Metro Transit Commission**	934-7928

North

• **Plymouth Metrolink**	349-7000
• **North Suburban Lines**	784-7196

Finally, you can call one of the following Dial-A-Ride Services. These are inexpensive taxi services that schedule on a first-come, first-served basis. Day-ahead reservations are encouraged, and you can order standing service. Your Dial-A-Ride driver can also give you a transfer ticket good for a bus ride. Call one of the following:

• **Anoka County Traveler**	323-5222
• **Columbia Heights Shared Ride**	422-7075
• **Hopkins Hop-A-Ride**	935-8003
• **Northeast and Lake Area Transit (National)**	644-8876
• **Plymouth Dial-A-Ride**	559-5057
• **Shakopee Dial-A-Ride**	445-9040
• **Southwest Metro Dial-A-Ride**	944-7126

Taxis

Unless you are in one of the two downtowns, at the airport, or perhaps in a few places such as Uptown and other commercial thoroughfares, you must telephone for a taxi rather than hailing one on the street. No problem, though, there are plenty here. Some only work in specific areas, so call the cab that covers your location.

Minneapolis

• **Blue & White Taxi**	333-3333
• **Minneapolis Yellow Cab**	824-4000

St. Paul

• **Citywide Cab**	489-1111
• **St. Paul Yellow Cab**	222-4433

Suburban

• **Minnesota Taxi, Inc.**	866-9999
• **Suburban Green & White Taxi**	222-2222

Minneapolis - St. Paul International Airport

Sooner or later you'll have to find your way in and out of the airport
(726-5555). By car, use the following routes:

- From Minneapolis and points north, take I-35W south to
  State Highway 62 east, or take Hiawatha Avenue all the way south.
- From St. Paul and points northeast, take I-35E south, then
  State Highway 5 west.
- From western, southern and eastern suburbs, take I-494 to
  State Highway 5.

Parking options:

- Short-term: $1/hour
- Long-term: $12/24 hours, $60/week
- Shuttle parking: $7/day, $35/week
- Heated underground valet parking: $15/hour in summer, $18/hour in
  winter

The following **bus routes** will take you to the airport:

- Minneapolis: from Nicollet Mall downtown, catch the 80 Express to
  the Mall of America. At the mall, take a 4, 7, or 15 to the airport.
- St. Paul: take the 54 Express from West 7th Street downtown directly to the airport.

You also have the option of hopping a hotel shuttle from one of the
downtowns directly to the airport. It costs more than a bus, but less than
a taxi. Call a major hotel in either downtown—they all run shuttles.
    Of course, you can always call a taxi.

Amtrak

The passenger station for Amtrak is centrally located in the Midway area
of St. Paul. The Empire Builder stops in the Twin Cities on its route from
Chicago (about 8 hours) to Seattle (48 hours plus).

- **Amtrak National Route Information**, 800-872-7245
- **Amtrak Twin Cities Passenger Station**, 730 Transfer Rd., St. Paul,
  644-1127

National Bus Services

The **Greyhound Bus Lines** national reservation number is
800-231-2222.

Greyhound has terminals in the following Twin Cities locations:

- **Minneapolis**, 29 N. 9th St., 371-3323
- **St. Paul**, 25 W. 7th St., 222-0509
- **International Airport**, 726-5118

There are also a number of regional bus lines you can use.

- **Jefferson Bus Lines** - Serves the southern part of the state, including Albert Lea, Austin, LaCrosse, Northfield, Red Wing, Rochester and Winona, as well as many U.S. cities further south, 332-3224.
- **Northfield Lines**, Inc. - Daily shuttles to Northfield, 339-3223.
- **Rochester Direct** - Daily shuttles between International Airport and Rochester, 725-0303.
- **Trailways** - Service to Dakotas and points west, 800-775-8974.

No matter how quickly you find your new home, you'll need a temporary place to stay in the Twin Cities, even if only for that first visit. Consider staying with a friend or relative for a short while as you get situated. If it's short term housing you're looking for consider a sublet, an option that's particularly open in the summer when colleges let out. The apartment search services listed in the "Apartment Hunting" chapter can assist in finding short-term leases while you search for a permanent living situation. Also, consider the following options, which vary in expense and accommodation.

Hotels and Motels

Rates are based on a single-bed room per night. Prices (often higher in the summer months) can vary depending on the season, and bargains can be had — often all you have to do is ask.

Minneapolis

- **American Inn**, 3924 Excelsior Blvd., St. Louis Park, 927-7731, $59.
- **Aqua City Motel**, 5739 Lyndale Ave. S., 861-6061,
  $45 with kitchenette.
- **Econo Lodge**, 2500 University Ave. SE, 331-6000, $55,
  $77 with kitchenette.
- **Gopher Campus Motor Lodge**, 925 4th St. SE, 331-3740, $49.50.
  Microwave ovens and refrigerators available.

St. Paul

- **Day's Inn Civic Center**, 175 W. 7th St., 292-8929, $78,
  refrigerators available.
- **Exel Inn**, I-94 at White Bear Ave., 771-5566, $59.
- **Northernaire Motel**, Hwy. 61 at Hwy. 36, 484-3336, $39,
  refrigerators and microwave ovens available, weekly discounts.

- **Twins Motor Inn**, 1975 University Ave. W., 645-0311, $49, weekly and monthly discounts.

Hostels

The City of Lakes International House (2400 Stevens Ave. S., Minneapolis, 871-3210), located among the Victorian homes near the Minneapolis Institute of Arts and convenient to downtown, offers private rooms with a group kitchen — for just $28 per night. The catch is that the hostel is only open to out-of-state and international visitors, and you will have to show identification to prove your non-Minnesotan status. There is no American Youth Hostel Association discount, though, since the City of Lakes House is independent.

Short-Term Leases

For a comfortable transition, the following leasing companies offer furnished rooms in convenient locations, such as downtown Minneapolis. Most apartments are equipped with linen, cooking utensils, and many other living needs.

- **Executive Suites**, 431 S. 7th St., Minneapolis, 339-9010; studios and one-bed apartments, equipped kitchens, weekly and monthly rates.
- **Midwest Guest Suites**, locations throughout the metro area; 735-8127; full suites, equipped kitchens, weekly and monthly rates.
- **Oakwood Corporate Housing**, locations throughout the Twin Cities, 800-897-4610; equipped and furnished suites, monthly rates.
- **Richfield Inn**, 7700 Bloomington Ave. S., Richfield, 869-3050; one- and two-bed apartments, short-term rates, equipped kitchens.

Bed & Breakfast Inns

If you don't mind the smell of potpourri, and you like cozy, try a bed & breakfast for your initial stay — an old-fashioned breakfast may even be included! The following rates are based on double occupancy for the most modest rooms available.

- **Chatsworth Bed & Breakfast**, 984 Ashland Ave., Saint Paul, 227-4288, $75.
- **DeSoto at Prior Bed & Breakfast**, 1522 DeSoto St., St. Paul, 774-2695, $69; discounts for multi-day visits and weekdays.
- **Le Blanc House**, 302 University Ave. NE, Minneapolis, 379-2570; $85.
- **1900 Dupont Bed & Breakfast**, 1900 Dupont Ave. S., Minneapolis, $69.

YMCAs and YWCAs

Unfortunately, none of the YMCAs or YWCAs in Minnesota offer lodgings. The downtown Minneapolis YMCA ended its rooms-for-rent service in the early 1990s as part of a remodeling of the facility.

Other Options

Hopefully, you'll be able to find an affordable and convenient place to stay from among these options. For other ideas, and to get a packet of information on a wide variety of local accommodations, contact the **Minnesota Office of Tourism** at **296-5029** or **800-657-3700**.

All area codes are in the 612 area code unless otherwise indicated.

Animals

Animal Bites 911

Minneapolis
Minneapolis Animal Control Shelter 348-4250
Animal Humane Society of Hennepin County 522-4325

St. Paul
St. Paul Animal Control Center 645-3953
Humane Society of Ramsey Co 645-7387
University of Minnesota Raptor Center 624-4745

Auto

Department of Public Safety - Motor Vehicle Division 296-6911
(License plates, state tabs, vehicle registration)

Minneapolis
Hennepin County Service Center/Vehicle Registration 348-8241

St. Paul
Midway Written Exam Station 642-0808
(If you have an out-of-state license.)

Birth/Death Certificates

Hennepin County Service Center (Minneapolis) 348-8241
St. Paul Health Center 292-7730
Minnesota Dept. of Health 623-5121
(for all MN counties, located on the U of M campus)

Child Abuse/Protection

Minneapolis
Hennepin County Child Abuse/Neglect (24 hour). 348-3552

St. Paul
Emergency Social Service (24 hour) 291-6795
Dakota County (to report). 891-7400
Ramsey Co. Child Protection (to report). 266-4500

City Government

Minneapolis
Assessor. 673-2387
Chamber of Commerce. 370-9132
City Clerk 673-2215
City Hall (general information) 673-3000
City Information Line (recording) 673-CITY
Mayor's Office. 673-2100
Minneapolis Community Development Agency 673-5095
Neighborhood Revitalization Program 673-5140

St. Paul
Chamber of Commerce. 223-5000
City Clerk 266-8989
City Hall (general information) 266-8500
Mayor's Office. 266-8510
Housing and Redevelopment Authority 266-6700
Residential Assessor 266-2141

Consumer Complaints and Services

Better Business Bureau of Minnesota. 699-1111
Minnesota Attorney General. 296-3353
United States Consumer Product Safety Office 290-3781
Minnesota Insurance Information Center 222-3800
Ramsey County Homestead Department. 266-2100

Crisis Hotlines

Crisis Connection (24 hour) 379-6363

Minneapolis
Crisis Intervention Center (24 hour) 347-3161
Minneapolis/Hennepin Co. Crisis Nursery (24 hr). 824-8000

St. Paul
Childrens Home Crisis Nurseries (24 hour) 646-4033
Crisis Intervention Center. 347-2222

Crisis Program (walk in) 221-8922
Emergency Social Service (24 hour) 291-6795
(for other crisis numbers see the white pages)

Disabled, Services for the

Epilepsy Foundation 800-779-0777
Minnesota State Council on Disability. 296-6785
Regional Service Center for Deaf and
Hard of Hearing People
    Voice 297-1316
    TTY 297-1313

Minneapolis
ARC Minnesota (Disability rights). 827-5641
Hennepin County Services for Persons With Disabilities 348-3440
(general information, referrals and intake)
Metropolitan Center for Independent Living 646-8342

St. Paul
ARC of Anoka and Ramsey Counties. 778-1414
Metro Mobility (to sign up). 221-0015
(transportation for the disabled)

Emergency

Ambulance. 911
Fire 911

Garbage

Minneapolis Solid Waste and Recycling. 673-2917
Ramsey County Solid Waste Residential Hotline 633-3279

Housing

Minnesota Tenant's Union 871-7485
St. Paul Tenants' Union 221-0501
US Department of Housing and Urban Development
  Housing Discrimination Hotline. 800-669-9777

Housing Code Violations

Minneapolis Department of Inspections: Housing. 673-5858
St. Paul. 266-9016

Municipal Housing Advice for Landlords and Tenants

Minneapolis Housing Services:. 673-3003
St. Paul Housing Information Office 266-6000

Immunization for Travel

Minneapolis. 625-1430
St. Paul 292-7746

Libraries (Main Numbers)

Metropolitan Library Service Agency 645-5731
Minneapolis Central Branch (general information) 372-6500
St. Paul Central Library (general information). 292-6311

Marriage Licenses

Hennepin County Service Center (Minneapolis). 348-8241
Ramsey County Vital Services Office (St. Paul) 266-8265

Parks

Minnesota State Park Reservations 800-246-2267

Police

Minneapolis
Emergency. 911
2nd Precinct (Downtown and Northeast) 673-5702
3rd Precinct (South) 673-5703
4th Precinct (North). 673-5704
5th Precinct (Southwest). 673-5705

St. Paul
Emergency. 911
St. Paul Police General Information 291-1111
Central District 292-3563
Eastern District 292-3565
Western District (North) 292-3512
Western District (South) 292-3549

Rape Crisis Services

Minneapolis
Rape and Sexual Assault Center (24 hour) 825-4357
Sexual Violence Center (24 hour). 871-5111

St. Paul
Sexual Offense Services (24 hour). 298-5898

Recycling

Minneapolis Solid Waste and Recycling. 673-2917
St. Paul Neighborhood Energy Consortium 644-7678

Roads

Road Condition Information 296-3076

Schools

Minneapolis School District 627-2050
St. Paul School District 293-5100

Sports

Minnesota Timberwolves 673-0900
Minnesota Twins 33-TWINS
Minnesota Vikings 333-8828
St. Paul Saints 644-6659
U of M Golden Gophers (all teams) 624-8080

State of Minnesota

Governors Office 296-3391
Information and Referral 296-6013

Street Maintenance

Minneapolis (24 hour) 673-5720
St. Paul (24 hour) 292-6600

Taxes

Minneapolis
Hennepin County Property Tax 348-3266

St. Paul
Ramsey County Property Tax 266-2000

State
Income Tax and Forms 296-3781
Taxpayers Rights Advocate 296-0992
Refund Status 296-4444
Special Taxes 297-1882

Federal
Income Tax Information 644-7515
Forms 800-829-3676

Taxis

Metro Area (including suburbs)
Minnesota Taxi Inc 866-9999
Suburban Green & White Taxi 222-2222

Minneapolis
Blue & White Taxi 333-3333
Minneapolis Yellow Cab 824-4000

St. Paul
Citywide Cab. 489-1111
St. Paul Yellow Taxi 222-4433

Time
Time 375-0830

Tourism
Minnesota Office of Tourism and Travel 800-657-3700
(locally) 296-5029

Transportation
Minneapolis - St. Paul International Airport. 726-5555
Holman Field - St. Paul. 224-4306
Amtrak 800-872-7245
St. Paul/Minneapolis Midway Amtrak Station 644-1127
Greyhound Bus Lines 800-231-2222
Metropolitan Council Transit Operations (Bus):
     Bus Route & Schedule Information 373-3333

Voting
Minneapolis. 673-2070
St. Paul 266-2171

Weather
Weather 375-0830

Zip Codes
Zip Code Information 349-4711

Entries in bold are chapter headings.

Maris Strautmanis has lived in Minneapolis and St. Paul for several years. He and his wife, Tamsie, can often be seen launching their canoe on Lake of the Isles. His experience as a newcomer begins with his parents, both of whom came to the United States from Latvia as children. A native of Wisconsin, Maris moved to Chicago, then Austin, Texas before returning to the Midwest. As a journalist, he has written for newspapers and a wire service. Currently, Maris is news director at a Twin Cities radio station. *The Newcomer's Handbook for Minneapolis-St. Paul* is his first book.

THE ORIGINAL, ALWAYS UPDATED, ABSOLUTELY INVALUABLE GUIDES FOR PEOPLE MOVING TO A CITY!

Find out about neigborhoods, apartment hunting, money matters, deposits/leases, getting settled, helpful services, shopping for the home, places of worship, belonging, sports/recreation, volunteering, green space, transportation, temporary lodgings and useful telephone numbers!

	# COPIES	TOTAL
Newcomer's Handbook™ for Atlanta	_____ x $13.95	$_____
Newcomer's Handbook™ for Boston	_____ x $13.95	$_____
Newcomer's Handbook™ for Chicago	_____ x $12.95	$_____
Newcomer's Handbook™ for Los Angeles	_____ x $13.95	$_____
Newcomer's Handbook™ for Minneapolis-St. Paul	_____ x $14.95	$_____
Newcomer's Handbook™ for New York City	_____ x $16.95	$_____
Newcomer's Handbook™ for San Francisco	_____ x $13.95	$_____
Newcomer's Handbook™ for Washington, DC	_____ x $13.95	$_____

SUBTOTAL $_____

TAX (IL residents add 8.75% sales tax) $_____

POSTAGE & HANDLING ($5.00 first book, $.75 each add'l) $_____

TOTAL $_____

SHIP TO:

_____
Name

_____
Title

_____
Company

_____
Address

_____ _____ _____
City   State   Zip

_____
Phone Number

Send this order form and a check or money order
payable to: First Books, Inc.

First Books, Inc., Mail Order Department
P.O. Box 578147, Chicago, IL 60657
773-276-5911

Allow 2-3 weeks for delivery.

DO YOU THINK YOU KNOW THE TWIN CITIES BETTER THAN WE DO? TELL US!

If you are the first to offer any new information about
Minneapolis-St. Paul that is subsequently used in the next
Newcomer's Handbook™ for Minneapolis-St.Paul,
we'll send you a free copy of our next edition.

SUGGESTIONS: _____

_____

_____

_____

_____

YOUR NAME: _____

YOUR ADDRESS: _____

_____

_____

Help keep this guide current. If a listing has changed, let us know.

UPDATES: _____

_____

_____

_____

_____

Send to: First Books, Inc.
P.O. Box 578147, Chicago, IL 60657

Smart Business Travel

HOW TO STAY SAFE WHEN YOU'RE ON THE ROAD

Don't be scared, be prepared!

"Offers great safety tips for the business traveler." – *Chicago Tribune*

"Handy"– *Frequent Flyer*

"Contains plenty of common sense"– *Los Angeles Times*

"Recommended"– *Houston Chronicle*

	# COPIES		TOTAL
Smart Business Travel	_____	× $12.95	$_____
TAX (IL residents add 8.75% sales tax)			$_____
POSTAGE & HANDLING ($3.00 first book, $.75 each add'l)			$_____
TOTAL			$_____

SHIP TO:

_____
Name

_____
Title

_____
Company

_____
Address

_____
City   State   Zip

_____
Phone Number

Send this order form and a check or money order
payable to First Books, Inc.

First Books, Inc. Mail Order Department
P.O. Box 578147, Chicago, IL 60657
773-276-5911

Allow 2-3 weeks for delivery.

Visit our web site at
http://www.firstbooks.com
for a sample of all our books.